BEHIND GLASS IN RUSSIA

1992

An Archaeologist's Journal

IAN W. BROWN

Behind Glass in Russia
1992

An Archaeologist's Journal

Ian W. Brown

ISBN 9781734573046

BORGO PUBLISHING

www.borgopublishing.com

Text and cover design, Borgo Publishing, Tuscaloosa, Alabama

Printed in the USA

Dedicated to Leo Tolstoy,
my personal guide to Russia

In quiet and untroubled times it seems to every administrator that it is only by his efforts that the whole population under his rule is kept going, and in this consciousness of being indispensable every administrator finds the chief reward of his labour and efforts. While the sea of history remains calm the ruler-administrator in his frail bark, holding on with a boat-hook to the ship of the people, and himself moving, naturally imagines that his efforts move the ship he is holding on to. But as soon as a storm arises and the sea begins to heave and the ship to move, such a delusion is no longer possible. The ship moves independently with its own enormous motion, the boat-hook no longer reaches the moving vessel, and suddenly the administrator, instead of appearing a ruler and a source of power, becomes an insignificant, useless, feeble man.

—LEO TOLSTOY, WAR AND PEACE

Leo Tolstoy (Trans. Louise and Aylmer Maude), *War and Peace* (Philadelphia: Franklin Library, 1981), 907.

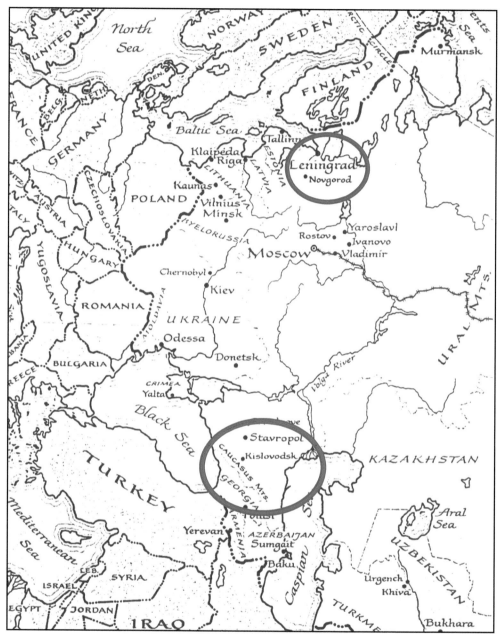

Figure 1. Map of the former U.S.S.R. showing the principal places visited by the People to People delegates. Leningrad is now St. Petersburg.

TABLE OF CONTENTS

FIGURES

1. Map of the former U.S.S.R. showing the principal places visited by the People to People delegates. Leningrad is now St. Petersburg.

2. The Pribaltiyskaya Hotel in St. Petersburg is surrounded by apartment buildings. Each morning the buses waited outside the hotel for the tourists.

3. A typical streetcar in St. Petersburg.

4. The Bronze Horseman—monument to Peter the Great.

5. Street vendors in small mobile units had become the norm in St. Petersburg shopping.

6. Igor Ashmaron, our Russian guide, explaining the history of the Peter and Paul Fortress.

7. Monument to Peter the Great by Mikhail Shemiakin, 1991.

8. Delegates confer with Russian archaeologists at the Institute for the History of Material Culture.

9. A display of Scythian artifacts at the Institute.

10. Kostienki I site plan, showing hearths relative to houses, circa 21,000 B.C.

11. Meals provided the delegates were out of this world, which contrasts with what the typical Russian citizen was eating.

12. Artifacts at the Peter the Great Museum are crammed into cases. The 18th-century geometric-style Chilkat blanket (probably Tlingit or Tsimshian Indian) shown here was nailed to the wall and folded to fit the case. It is one of the rarest objects of its kind in the world.

13. Tlingit warrior diorama in the Peter the Great Museum.

14. The author enjoying the canal tour.

15. Late 15th-century reconstructed fortifications at Old Ladoga.

16. The excavated tower shows stabilization methods.

17. Within the fortress walls is St. George Cathedral, built circa A.D.1165.

18. A picnic lunch atop one of the kurgans north of Old Ladoga on the Volhov River.

44. One of the kremlin's towers near the excavations. Note the giant arches for support, as well as the wide platform on the ramparts.

45. Construction of the 15th-century fortifications at Novgorod. A brick facade hides a thick layer of stone rubble.

46. The interior wall of the kremlin is to the right. The Detinets restaurant, the scene of our wonderful meal, occurs in the background.

47. A trench through the kremlin's fortifications. The timber walls date to the 11th-13th centuries. They were then neatly stacked and used as a base for the brick and rubble walls erected in the 1490s. Clay was excavated from the moat and packed around the logs to keep them from shifting.

48. The weight of the stone fortification depressed the underlying soil and wood foundation.

49. Beach in front of the Yuriev Monastery, Novgorod.

50. The Yuriev Monastery and Cathedral. This translates as the St. George Cathedral.

51. Vendors selling their wares outside the monastery and cathedral grounds.

52. Delegates gather at the entrance to the Yuriev Monastery and Cathedral.

53. Interior of the Yuriev Monastery. Russians have a great love for flowers.

54. The Yuriev Cathedral has onion-shaped cupolas, which replaced dome-shaped ones in the late 17th century. This cathedral once had the third largest number of icons in Novgorod and has wonderful acoustics.

55. Examples of the frescos within the Yuriev Cathedral.

56. A painting in the interior of the Yuriev Cathedral cupola.

57. Entrance sign to the Vitoslavlitsy Museum of Wooden Architecture in Novgorod. Churches and houses were moved here from all parts of the region.

58. This is a typical house of the 1870s. Despite its size, there is actually very little living space in the structure. Most of the house is used for livestock and workshops.

59. A schematic drawing of the house in Figure 58.

60. A kitchen in the same house.

61. The second-floor workshop, also in the same house.

62. Two large wooden churches on the grounds. The Church of Peredki (1599) is on the left and the Octagonal Church (1757) is on the right.

63. A close-up view of the unusual joints of the Octagonal Church.

64. The Church of Peredki is immense.

65. To the right of the Church of Peredki is the Peasant Cottage of Izba.

66. The Peasant Cottage has double saddle joints.

67. Another church at the Vitoslavlitsy Museum.

68. Another highly decorative church on the grounds.

69. The church in Figure 68 has squared joints and a railing with geometric cutouts.

70. The only "living" parts of the Vitoslavlitsy Museum are its gardens.

71. Children of any time seem to enjoy swings.

72. The Museum of Musical Instruments had only recently been established when we visited Novgorod.

73. The Resort Moscow Hotel is considered to be one of the finest hotels in the country.

74. A market located near the hotel.

75. This area is the mineral water capital of Russia and is a great retreat for those who vacation. Summer homes in the mountains are quite common.

76. Sketch of the Klin-Yar site, a Koban-Alan culture settlement and cemetery west of Kislovodsk.

77. The Klin-Yar site of the Koban-Alanian culture is located in a very strategic position. The high foundation for the fortress appears in the middle distance to the left. This settlement was situated along the Great Silk Road.

78. The location of the catacombs excavation relative to the fortified settlement on top of the promontory.

79. Delegates approach the Klin-Yar catacombs excavation. The tombs date to the Iron and early Middle Ages.

80. The smaller tomb located within the excavated area.

81. Deep excavations in the catacombs revealed burials of the Alanian culture dating to the fourth century A.D.

82. A stone blocks the passageway to the burial chamber and the exposed skeleton. This particular tomb was used only once.

83. A very deep shaft led to the larger tomb, believed to be about 5 m. below the present surface.

84. A more detailed sketch of the fortress at the Klin-Yar site, a medieval fortification of the Alanian culture.

85. The cliff leading to the fortress was approachable in places, but it still would have been a major deterrent to invaders.

86. Delegates face east on this very narrow promontory, but it served its purpose as a fortress. It was of Alanian culture design and dated from the sixth-ninth centuries A.D.

87.   This view along the fortified promontory is to the south. The road that can be seen to the right in the middle-distance wraps around the site.

88.   The current road has probably been situated in the same place for millennia as part of the Silk Road. The caves in the cliffs are still used to fence in livestock.

89.   Haystacks and livestock dot the landscape of the ancient Alanians.

90.   Site of the fortress overlooking Honey Water Falls.

91.   Sketch of the Alanian fortress at Honey Water Falls.

92.   The only access to the interior of the fortifications was a narrow fissure in the rock.

93.   View of Honey Water Falls from the fortified site.

94.   The Love and Treason Castle.

95.   The cliffs above the castle, scene of the treachery.

96.   The restaurant at the Love and Treason Castle was reported to have the finest meals in southern Russia—we all agreed.

97.   Transportation in the Northern Caucasus was by military helicopters.

98.   Aerial view of a kurgan in the steppes, the Vorovskolesskoe settlement.

99.   The Vorovskolesskoe kurgan, as seen from the ground.

100.   Vladimira Petrenko lectures on the Vorovskolesskoe settlement. It consists of dozens of kurgans dating to the Maikop culture of five to four thousand years ago.

101.   From the top of one of the kurgans two others can be seen in the middle distance.

102.   Because of privatization, looting had become a major problem. The government could no longer give adequate protection to sites.

103.   Sketch of the Razdolnoje site, a Scythian burial mound dating to the fourth-third centuries B.C.

104.   Generalized section drawing of the Razdolnoje site burial mound.

105.   About half of the overlying mound at the Razdolnoje site had been excavated.

106.   View of the east side of the balk, showing a certain amount of complexity to the mound construction.

107.   Andrew Belinski (left) and Yuri N. Litvinenko lecture on the site excavations. A stone ring on a raised platform encircles the burial chambers, which are marked by clusters of stones.

108.   Vladimira Petrenko and Sergei Korenevsky take a closer look at the stratigraphy.

INTRODUCTION

IN JUNE OF 1992 I RECEIVED A LETTER FROM PEOPLE TO PEOPLE, A CITIZEN AMBASSAdor Program whose headquarters are located in Seattle, Washington. The letter invited me to be a part of a team of archaeology delegates to make the first tour of the former Soviet Union since Perestroika began. I was flattered, but upon seeing that the price was just shy of $5,000, I promptly threw the invitation into the trash can. I then went about my daily business, but my thoughts kept returning to the letter and what an honor it was to be invited. I had had a single course on Central Asia archaeology when I was an undergraduate, so I did know a little (very little) of at least one of the areas on the planned trip. I also knew about the medieval city of Novgorod from introductory archaeology courses. It was hard not to have remembered the wonderful preservation of wood and other organic remains from this important community in northern Russia. With these thoughts running through my head, I returned to the trash and resurrected the somewhat crumpled invitation.

The following day I asked James D. Yarbrough, the Dean of the College of Arts and Sciences, if there were any funds available at the University of Alabama where I was employed to support travel of this nature. I was told money was limited, as I already knew, but if I was able to raise all the other funds Arts and Sciences would put $500 toward the trip. That sounded the challenge! I immediately solicited other programs, departments, and offices on campus to see if there were any other funding possibilities. As it turned out, there were. Almost all of those who were asked contributed something, some large some small, but all very much appreciated. Eventually, when I surpassed the halfway mark, Douglas E. Jones, Director of the Alabama Museum of Natural History, where I held a curatorial appointment, generously contributed the remaining half. Much to my surprise and pleasure, the trip was on, but then it hit me what a dilemma I faced. When I first started applying for travel funds, I mainly wanted my university to know that this was not a distinction for me personally to have been asked, but it was also an honor for the university for me to go. With that said, I didn't really think that it was going to happen!

The summer of 1992 was a particularly busy time for me. Although I was not in the field that season, I was deeply involved in writing a synthesis article on the past five years of Southeastern U.S. archaeology, and this project was about to do me in.[1] Moreover, I was up for tenure and promotion that year and my dossier had to be signed, sealed, and delivered to the Dean by October 1. As the 16-day trip to Russia was to begin September 20, there was no way I could return to the dossier task later. I was also chairing the Mentoring Program at the university, which was in its first year of operation, so there were many responsibilities in August in getting this program started. As my wife's 40th birthday was on September 30, I also had considerable guilt about missing this important occasion, so I wanted to make sure I threw a surprise party for her before leaving. I was concerned about my inability to prepare adequately for the trip, but my greatest anguish came from the fact that I knew little about Russia's past or present. What kind of representative would I be going into a land where I lacked an appreciation of its people? My only hope was that there might be a few others like me. Knowing little about Russian society and culture, I decided to concentrate on the land. It was a People to People delegation, but as I knew not a stick of the Russian language (and still don't beyond a half dozen phrases), I resigned myself to the fact that I would merely be a traveler to a new landscape. I wanted to see Russia and if I also got to meet some Russians in the process, so much the better. I certainly didn't anticipate that any friendships would develop from this encounter, so I was pleasantly surprised when they did. One thing I learned from this trip is that it is impossible for a person trained in anthropology to study the land apart from its people, even on a two-week "vacation."

As stated, I am an anthropologist, one who specializes in the archaeology of the Southeastern U.S. In touring locations from St. Petersburg to Novgorod to the Northern Caucasus we were exposed to a deluge of information from numerous Russian archaeologists. Many of them had studied English and, to my embarrassment concerning my own linguistic inabilities, were quite fluent in it. Others could not speak English, so we relied heavily on interpreters. Our three main guides—Albert, Alona, and Igor—were exceptional both as interpreters and as people.[2] They made the trip a true delight. However, they were unfamil-

---

1 Ian W. Brown, "Recent Trends in the Archaeology of the Southeastern United States," *Journal of Archaeological Research* 2, no. 1 (1994): 45-111.

2 Albert Yakimovsky, Alona Tchistyakova, and Igor (Gary) Ashmaron.

iar with the technological language of archaeology and I am not so sure that all the messages translated correctly. Moreover, as we were moving at such a hectic pace, I am not totally confident in my own comprehension and recording of all that was said. I did make an earnest attempt to check and recheck names, dates, and historical information, but it would be unusually lucky and fortunate if I recorded everything accurately. I did the best that I could do under the circumstances and will leave it to scholars of Russia's past and present to critique.

Although I hope that the information presented here is factually correct, perhaps of more significance for anyone going to Russia today is my personal account of what I saw at the time I saw it. This volume is my journal. I have maintained a continuous daily journal for 43 years and, consequently, have always had good practice in writing fast. During the course of each day I kept notes in a small black notebook, which became the main tool for stirring my memory at the end of the day. My entries were written either in the evening following the day's activities or during the morning immediately thereafter, so they are basically instantaneous accounts. This has value in terms of the accuracy of the record, I hope, but this daily routine did not allow time for much reflection, especially considering the rapid pace of our travels. It is usually valuable to see, listen, learn, digest, and then reflect on one's environment (cultural and physical), but there was no time on this trip for such contemplation. My great fear was that if I did not record events as I was living them, I would be totally unable to label photographs later on. Considering that I shot over 16 rolls of film on the trip, this was a legitimate fear.

As with any personal journal, there are a number of statements made which I prefer not to share. One cannot live for 16 days with over 40 people and not have some unsociable things to say on occasion. And I am sure that I have been on the receiving end in other people's logs. Not wishing to embarrass specific individuals, or myself, I have deleted certain items from the final text. When such deletions occur, gaps are indicated by the following notation [...]. I have also deleted passages that relate to my own specific research interests or personal matters and are unnecessary details. I assume that these passages are of no interest to anyone but myself and, by virtue of their being left out, the reader is left in the dark as to whether I am being unduly scholarly or simply disagreeable—I prefer it that way.

My trip and, consequently, this volume was supported by grants from the Alabama Museum of Natural History, the Alabama Natural History Society, the University of Alabama's President's Office, the Office of Sponsored Programs, the Dean's Office of the College of Arts and Sciences, the Department of Anthropology, and Capstone International (a program at the University of Alabama). I would especially like to thank E. Culpepper Clark, Richard A. Diehl, Pamela Hisey, Douglas E. Jones, Stanley T. Jones, Edward H. Moseley, E. Roger Sayers, Robert L. Wells, and James D. Yarbrough. On the trip itself both I and the members of the delegation overall owed much to the leadership and guidance of Shereen A. Lerner (delegation leader) and Paul Bristo (People to People Courier). Many of my fellow delegates became friends at the time, and some have persisted for many a year. With the fear of leaving some one out, I would nevertheless like to mention my comrades on this wonderful trip: Lysbeth B. (Beth) Acuff, Maria Susana Azzi, Ele A. (Tony) Baker, Colleen M. Beck, Cory D. Breternitz, Gillian S. Brooks, Jeffrey V. Buechler, Scott L. Carpenter, Susan M. Collins, John B. Cornell, Frederick G. Dreier, Sandra Jo Forney, Joel W. Grossman, John W. Hohmann, Karlene Jones-Bley, Rebecca S. Lange, Aminta D. Lara-Peters, Judith V. Lelchook, Laura L. Longmore (Edwards), Janet S. Pollak, Elizabeth A. Ragan, Diane L. Rhodes, Lance W. Rom, Michael R. Selle, M. Kay Shelton, Jack E. Smith, Jerry J. Stipp, David W. Valentine, Christy L. Wells, Adrian S. White, Joyce A. Williams, Randy S. Willimann, and Thomas C. Windes. I owe a special debt to Yuri N. Litvinenko who read and commented on an initial draft of this work, which I composed immediately upon arriving home. My wife, Easty Lambert-Brown, appears under the name Nancy at various places in the journal. They are one in the same, Easty being a family name that she revived in 2012. She was kind enough to help make my journal drawings presentable, for which I am most grateful.

There is one final issue—why now? That is not a simple question to answer. I could make up all sorts of excuses, but the main reason has to do with time. I retired from the University of Alabama on June 1, 2020, after having spent just shy of 30 years as a professor. I remain as Professor Emeritus, as well as Curator Emeritus with the museum, but no longer having to teach or do administrative work has provided me with the luxury of time to myself. Over the past several months I have "pounded the keys" typing away at various documents, mostly extracts from my journal of adventures that I thought might be of a larger interest than to me alone. This is, pure and simple, my motivation for finally publishing *Behind Glass in Russian 1992, an Archaeologist's Journal.*

AN ARCHAEOLOGIST'S JOURNAL

...HAD A NICE FLIGHT TO ATLANTA AND THEN NEW YORK. IT WAS ESPECIALLY PRETTY flying into New York. All the lights, all the miniature cars forming a constant stream on the highways. A line of ants is the only appropriate imagery. But they cooperate. They lock jaws and proceed along the line carrying food and messages back and forth. As cars exited and entered the highways it was clear there was no cooperation among men. Each was going on his own way—somewhere— where could they be going?

I had no hassles in collecting my bag/case and, fortunately, catching the shuttle to JFK ran relatively smoothly also. Airport life in New York is depressing. As I emerged from the baggage claim area about a half dozen taxi drivers surrounded me outside. Each wanted to take me somewhere in the city—anywhere. We had been warned about independents, so I said thanks, but no thanks. Each looked sleazy and bitter, walking back and forth between people with bags trying to convince them they were legitimate. I'm not so sure that the smelly bus that I ended up in was any more legitimate than the taxis. LaGuardia is so dirty, at least on the outside. And what a contrast. As I sat on the bus, I witnessed the mass of humanity beyond the glass—all in black and white, scurrying around trying to make a living. Some were guiding the clean folk out of the building into safe "clean" transports. Others were scurrying, trying to convince the same folk that there's an alternative way. It may be more expensive, it may not be as safe, but it was different and it may be worth experiencing. Also there were the derelicts. They wore suit coats, ragged around the edges, to match their scuffed shoes. They were relatively clean, with slicked black hair, but you could tell their occupation from their ambling. They walk slowly down the streets eyeing baggage, constantly looking for the opportunity to enhance their own lives.

All of this occurs in black and white beneath the night air. And inside there is color. The air is fresher, there are far fewer people, the airline people are neatly dressed in spanking clean suits, and everyone smiles. All this separated by a one-inch glass. What horror there would be if the glass was suddenly lifted. I wonder who would be the first to cross the invisible line. I wonder who would be more horrified.

September 19, 1992 (Saturday)

New York life.

I proceeded on to the JFK Holiday Inn, taking another shuttle from the airport. My turn to be horrified when I learned that the bill was $140!! I thought I had died and gone to hell. At first, I paid it in cash, but thought otherwise later as I would lack money in Russia. Came back downstairs and put it on my new American Express Corporate Card. At least it will be good for something. The room was beautiful though, with nice thick glass, relatively soundproof too. A berth on the 10th floor offered added protection, as did a security fence that encircled the hotel, complete with guard. I do hope in Russia that I will not be so apprehensive about going outside.

HOW DO I BEGIN? I'M WRITING AT 7 P.M. ON MONDAY, HAVING SLEPT ONLY ABOUT an hour or so in the last 35 hours, so my mind is not running smoothly. I have to force myself to stay up as long as possible though, so that I will not fall victim to jet lag.

I met all the other delegates yesterday at 11:30 a.m. We met over cocktails (I just drank juice and lots of it) and tried to lock jaws, determining who knew whose friends so that linkages could be made. After a meal (our last greens we were told) we had various talks on what to expect: the dos and don'ts. Then we got on Finnair and headed for Helsinki. I sat next to John Hohmann,[3] a nice guy from Phoenix. I tried hard to sleep on the plane. It was a smooth ride, but I just couldn't sleep, despite the eyeshades. Before I knew it, the sunrise was upon us and we landed in Finland. How beautiful it is from the air, the land of a thousand lakes. Everywhere there were little clusters of rural houses, many with red roofs, and so very neat. The airport matched the aerial view in the neat, clean, new appearance. As the sun shone brightly, everything seemed sound in Finland.

In descending to St. Petersburg we entered a fog, which turned to a light drizzle. And we never came out of it. Everything turned to black and white. Some men in military uniform stood at the ramp to our plane. They didn't say anything, and they didn't seem to be particularly interested in us, but clearly they had to be there. A short while later another plane landed, and I saw that there was a group of soldiers to "greet" them too. We piled into a dilapidated caravan that carted us, like cattle, to the equally dilapidated terminal. Our guide, Paul Bristol, assured us that they had done major renovation at it since he was there in the spring, but it was difficult to tell whether the plaster was decaying or only half put on. We met our Russian guides after going through customs, a very easy process, and we piled into a smelly bus and headed to the city. Everything smelled like coal and oil mixed with some sort of greasy food smell, which I can't distinguish. All the way to St. Petersburg we saw buildings in decay, lots of soldiers, lots of military vehicles, all of which looked in need of repair. A wall

---

3 In 1992 Dr. Hohmann was Chief Archaeologist of the Western Regional Office of Louis Berger and Associates, Inc., a major cultural resource management firm.

or two of rickety scaffolding was the only indication that repair was intended for many of the structures. The people, all dressed in Western clothes, totally indistinguishable from in New York, either walked rapidly along the street or clustered in groups. The groups consisted of four or five in a circle discussing some subject, or a line in front of a door or portable shop. These "shops," about 6 x 3 feet were arranged on the pavement in front of stores, now closed. All of them were doing a brisk business, probably in black market items. There were no smiles, except occasionally among the young lovers who walked arm in arm. And lots of scruffy young kids, unmonitored by adults, and scurrying among the crowd with some purpose of their own. There was no filth, no trash, no litter, no uncollected garbage, but there was decay everywhere. And this is not the kind of decay that has happened in the last two years, or even in the last 10 years. The buildings are just being allowed to fall apart and, in time, they will do just that. I had hoped that this would improve as we entered the old city of St. Petersburg. There was more effort there, to be sure, but was not enough to make a major effect in stalling the death of this city.

Eventually, next to the sea we entered a complex of high-rise apartment buildings that literally hold thousands of people. They, too, are shabby, clearly

Figure 2.
The Pribaltiyskaya Hotel in St. Petersburg is surrounded by apartment buildings. Each morning the buses waited outside the hotel for the tourists.

run down on the outside, with all sorts of junk put out on the "porches." The junk were the unworkables, objects that were potentially too valuable, even in their non-functioning state, to be discarded. These complexes formed a ring around a higher, cleaner, more architecturally sound and ornate building, which turned out to be our hotel "The Pribaltiyskaya." I was embarrassed and ashamed. How could they have put this comparatively beautiful hotel in the midst of thousands of windows, windows filled with envious eyes? And how could I nonchalantly descend the bus and ascend the high flight of stairs to such bourgeois decadence? Why did they make it such a monument among the masses? It seems such a non-Soviet thing to have done.

We were accosted by teenagers in front of the hotel. Some had sheaths of medals and buttons; others had short

Figure 3.
A typical streetcar in St. Petersburg.

Figure 4.
The Bronze Horseman— monument to Peter the Great.

Figure 5.
Street vendors in small mobile units had become the norm in St. Petersburg shopping.

poles wrapped with watches. And none were hesitant about stepping right up to your face. In the hotel lobby we got our room assignment. I'm alone because my roommate cancelled out. That's okay with me, but I do hope I do not have to pay extra. There were several prostitutes sitting in chairs along the walls, usually with some papers in their laps. They did not come after us, as we had been warned, but they were awaiting eye contact.

We dropped off things in our rooms, did a quick cleanup, and then met the bus. Did a tour of the central city and also ate lunch (at 3 p.m.!). The most memorable stops were the meal, the Saints Peter and Paul Cathedral, and the Russian Orthodox Church. For the meal we entered a dark, dingy private restaurant, "welcomed" by a stone-faced doorman. We walked up two flights of stone stairs until we came to our room. Along the way were little rooms off to the left and right with one or two people in each either sitting there staring at us or doing something unidentifiable. We sat in a big "U" in a small room, with each of our chairs squeezed together. "Dinner" consisted of an appetizer of jellied meat, vegetable soup, a steak dish with potatoes and squash, and ice cream. It was much more than I expected.

We hustled out of there into the bus and off to the Peter and Paul Fortress. There I was confronted with a hoard of dirty ruffians straight out of Dickens, and these six to nine-year-olds were persistent. They wanted money. I managed to get by them and into the fortress, but only by the skin of my teeth. What amazed me was the cathedral. There were the coffins of Peter the Great, Catherine the Great, and all the other Emperors and members of the Royal family. There they were in a dilapidated building which is making great strides on the inside, but which shared the same decay outside. Not long ago there was noth-

Figure 6.
Igor Ashmaron, our Russian guide, explaining the history of the Peter and Paul Fortress.

Figure 7.
Monument to Peter the Great by Mikhail Shemiakin, 1991.

ing on the inside at all, so they are making progress in rebuilding their history. But they haven't learned. When we passed a giant statue of Lenin our guide sounded quite pleased when he said that it will soon be taken down, with the metal to be used for other things. Once again, they are erasing history, whether good or bad these things are historical materials and should be preserved.

Finally, before returning to the hotel we visited a Russian Orthodox service. Dozens of short plump grandmother figures, or babushkas, devotedly and sometimes angrily at our presence, lit their candles and said their voluminous prayers. We listened to the beautiful music, but it meant a lot more before we learned that they are professional singers hired by the state to perform. Too much artificial here as yet. I need to find the reality.

Went back to the hotel, picked up a bottle of mineral water for my ablutions, wrapped a bar of soap and a dollar bill for my floor lady, and put the chain on my door, as per suggested. This is reality on the daily level.

September 22, 1992
(Tuesday)

A breakfast experience.

**Institute for the History
of Material Culture in
St. Petersburg.**

**The people:
scientists, general
citizens, and
prostitutes.**

Russian ballet.

Some color seeped into St. Petersburg today, although it did not come quickly or willingly. I started off the morning very bad. Slept solidly for several hours and then woke up around 1 a.m. Closed my eyes and was up again at 2 a.m., then 3 a.m. This was ridiculous. I never pack an alarm clock because of my biological one, but it had gone absolutely haywire. Was up again at 4 a.m., wide awake, but refused to get up or I would never get over jet lag. Scheduled myself for 6 a.m. and next opened my eyes at 8:25 a.m. I couldn't believe it! Had only five minutes to get ready for breakfast. I was so mad at myself.

Got down to the breakfast area—the Pushkin Room, at 8:40 a.m., but shouldn't have worried. Everyone was in the hall awaiting an empty room. Turns out that another group had gone into our dining area and there was no one watching out for it. People seem to be pretty much at ease about it though. We have a good group. We finally ended up in the cafeteria. The food truly is an experience. Lots of cold cuts, some egg-like things that were either hard boiled or in scrambled squares that look like custard, lots of relish-like dishes that are a bit hard to take in the morning, grits/oatmeal like substance (which is neither nor) and tea. Ah, the tea. That is something refreshingly familiar. The food will grow on me but hasn't yet.

Waded through the young boys hawking their wares and ascended the bus to the Institute for the History of Material Culture, formerly the Institute of Archaeology, Leningrad Branch. Everyone looks at us in the bus, not just because it is newer and neater than the city buses, but there is space in ours. Every bus we pass has more people standing than sitting, with faces pressed against the windows. They come so close as we pass on the street that I feel embarrassed and have difficulty meeting their stares.

At the Institute we entered a long narrow door that opens almost immediately on a busy street fronting the river and the Peter and Paul Fortress. Apparently, the building we are in was owned and erected by an Italian family, and that is clearly seen in the decor—highly ornate with giant unlit chandeliers. It is a house that craves for light, but the doors and windows are shut and only small scattered lamps offer means for getting around. Everything is stone. To get to our room we walk through a long tall amply lit corridor, much like a fissure leading into a cave. Along the walls are "exhibits," photo displays and drawings of archaeological findings arranged by what appear to be cultural periods. Offices come off the halls and at the end of it is a conference room where we sat. This is a long narrow room, again highly ornate. Windows open to the river with a magnificent view of the Saints Peter and Paul Cathedral, but we did not discover this until later. Again, everything is closed up, stuffy, with the same somewhat greasy smell which pervades everywhere. We sat in two columns of chairs with a narrow aisle in the middle and on the left. Each row of chairs consisted of six or seven seats that were attached. The whole row could be moved, which is good because they were tightly jammed together. The seats themselves are true booby traps. If you happen to be sitting in one with your feet on the raised area on the seat before you, they will be neatly guillotined if someone elects to sit down. I sat in the second row on the left.

Professor V. M. Masson, Director of the Institute, began the proceedings, welcoming us and telling us something about the recent history and purposes of the Institute. He is quite a presence. He stands over 6 feet tall, with a large body and formidable head. The thick glasses provide a barrier and it is not clear that he focuses on anyone, as his loud pounding voice hammers away at the audience. He gave his introduction in English, which was very courteous to us, but I believe we would have learned more had it been translated...

After his introduction, marred by a projector that just would not cooperate, and slides that were of poor quality, we took a little break. The cord leading up to the slide projector was cloth-wrapped. I hadn't seen one like that since I was a child. I believe they have been banned in the States because of fire hazard. I am truly amazed that this is a superpower. All of their effort and money went into the military, so much of the other parts of life were neglected. But the people have done well with what they have, that is clear.

I met Prof. Masson during the break. I brought him greetings from Karl (Lamberg-Karlovsky)[4] and said what a pleasure it was to meet him, having read his book on Central Asia as one of my first books in archaeology.[5] He seemed

---

4   C. C. Lamberg-Karlosky was a Professor in the Department of Anthropology at the time of my trip to Russia and is now Professor Emeritus. When I was on the staff of Harvard's Peabody Museum in the 1980s, Prof. Lamberg-Karlovsky was its Director. I served as his Assistant Director in 1989-90.

5   V. M. Masson and V. I. Sarianidi, *Central Asia: Turkmenia Before the Achaemenids* (London: Thames & Hudson Ltd., 1972).

pleased, but he is a man on the run. No matter who he was speaking to, he was looking elsewhere and trying to move on.

Fred Dreier[6] gave a talk on early peopling of the New World. His focus was on the Archaic skeletal structure of some historic Indian groups in California. He seemed to be saying these people were closer to Neanderthal than modern humans, which I found to be astonishing. Not that these variations are not something that require explanation, but I was horrified that, as a delegation, we might be giving the impression that Americans are accepting this idea. As he himself mentioned Old Crow Flats and failed to mention that the caribou flesher now dates to a couple of thousand years ago max, I did discuss this following his talk. I just wanted to give the Russian folk some sense that not all of us were in agreement with the speculations presented by Dr. Dreier, but I hope I did it in a respectful non-combative manner. I did go up to Fred later, said how interesting his work was, and urged him to find reasons for these strange finds. I didn't want to be an ass over this, but I was a bit embarrassed by the content of the presentation and something had to be said. Enough.

Before lunch we heard Dr. Sergei N. Astakhov[7] give a presentation on Palaeolithic sites in Siberia. Fascinating information, very informative talk. I signed up to visit his department tomorrow, as of all the archaeology in Russia I probably know more (or at least been exposed more) to the early remains. It would be nice to actually see the material I have read about for years.

We went back to the same restaurant we ate at yesterday (wish I could describe where and what name, but I know it is relatively close to the Institute and along a side street to a busy thoroughfare). The tables were set up differently, isolated rather than in a big U, so that was nice because it gave us more room. Dr. Astakhov sat at our table and was very pleasant to talk with.

We went back to the Institute and heard Dr. G. N. Kurochkin talk about Scythian finds. Some spectacular discoveries are coming out of the burial tombs and it was nice to be brought up to date on them.[8] When he was finished, and

---

6 At the time of our trip, Dr. Dreier was a teacher at Red Bluff Union High School in Red Bluff, California and an Instructor at Shasta Community College, also in Red Bluff.

7 Dr. Astakhov was on the staff of the Institute for the History of Material Culture, St. Petersburg.

8 See also G.N. Kurochkin, "Archeological Search for the Near Eastern Aryans and the Royal Cemetery of Marlik in Northern Iran," Annales Academiae Scientiarum Fennicae, Series B, 271, no. 1 (1993): 389–395.

all questions asked, I was astonished to see that it was 4:30 p.m. Only half an hour to dinner, and we had just finished eating! I'm going to be a roly-poly by the time I leave here.

We got back to the hotel with just enough time to freshen up. Passed the hookers on the way and managed not to avoid eye contact. How could I help it? They are truly some of the most beautiful women I have ever seen. One blonde lady, with a tight form-fitting black dress, complete with dangling black balls along the hem, could have been featured in *Playboy.* And she had the face and eyes of an angel. As mine met hers I could see a light in hers, gently questioning me whether I was interested. Of course I was interested. How could one be in-different to such beauty. In fact, the most beautiful things I have seen thus far are the prostitutes, perfectly willing to give a piece of that beauty, their youth and pride, for some hard currency. I felt ashamed, not for them, but for me.

We had a nice light meal and then went down to the buses, continuing our drive around St. Petersburg on the way to the theatre. The sun was still out, and I thought about how beautiful St. Petersburg is in the sunlight. The rot of the buildings is not half so visible; the parks, though overgrown, both brighter and more inviting; and the litter-less streets look as if there is greater care that I detected yesterday. There are no vagrants—imagine, a city with five million and I saw no homeless. Plenty of people are hawking their wares, but no one is panhandling. At night the streets are empty, except for the couples. Everyone is "home" somewhere, protected by their large extended family. They might be in a room with 12 others, but they have a roof overhead and share blood with their roommates. I saw no fear in the eyes of those walking the streets. They seemed secure—no gangs of young boys, no evidence of drug pushing, no violence to speak of, no hookers there. What would be the sense? The money is in the for-eigner's hotels, not in the streets.

What an evening. We attended the St. Petersburg Russian Ballet performance of Swan Lake. A marvelous theatre, very plush on the inside with giant circular walls at least four stories of balconies high encircling the floor. We sat on the left fairly close to the stage and orchestra. The performance overall was marvelous, and I kept thinking how much my mother would enjoy it. I need to know more about ballet though. After the second curtain, when they brought out the flow-ers, I and several others descended to the bus. After a while of chatting we be-came aware that the crowds had not emerged. Rather shamefacedly we skulked back into the theatre and sat down to enjoy the third act, having profited considerably from our stint in the night air. We got home around 10:45 p.m., shopped a little in the hotel store, noted that all the ladies were snug in bed, and I headed for mine. Settled down with Tolstoy's *The Cossacks*[9] and drifted off to sleep.

---

9 Lyov Tolstoy, *The Cossacks* (New York: P. F. Collier & Son, 1887).

EVERYTHING WENT SMOOTHLY THIS MORNING. WE HAD A NICE BREAKFAST OF wonderful pastries and oatmeal. This is the first real oatmeal I've had I think, and it was delicious. We then went back to the Institute and started the session with a talk by Shereen (Lerner).[10] She was not able to give her talk yesterday because Dr. Masson dominated. She spoke about the goals and objectives of People to People and I think it was well received by the Russians. It was very clear to us, but it's not always so clear that the Russians know why we are here.

John Hohmann gave an excellent talk on the discoveries at and the preservation of the Casa Malpais site in northeast Arizona. It fascinated all of us and was presented in a nice comprehensible fashion to our hosts. The site itself seems to be single component and built relatively fast around A.D. 1268. There is a large pueblo structure of at least three stories of square rooms in places and an associated rectangular kiva. In one part of the pueblo are two levels of underground chambers. These and a large portion of the pueblo itself seem to be ceremonially related because of the objects found within them. In the underground chambers were discovered large pots and shrines, which had within them quartz crystals, turquoise, eagle feathers, lots of copper from the Aztecs, and even tiny Clovis points. Three of the latter have been found and they were of local material probably secured from nearby sites. Obviously, they were found, deemed of interest, and put within the shrine, America's first museum. Tremendous preservation. Nearby they discovered natural fissures in the rocks, which they descended into by ropes and found burial chambers. Some of the chambers were as big as the room we were in. In a room that size there could be as many as 73 individuals, and always adults. There were no children and so they don't really know who those people were in terms of status. There were many chambers, and each was subdivided into small crypts that held between one and four individuals. These crypts were used repeatedly but the Indians did not disturb those that were already deposited. There have been both Hopi and Zuni claims to the burials and site. They cannot show the burials or publish the material in detail until this is

More on the Institute: talks and meetings.

Peter the Great Museum of Anthropology.

A canal trip and a new friendship.

---

10   As noted in the Introduction, Dr. Lerner was the Delegation Leader. Her official title at the time was State Historic Preservation Officer at the Arizona State Parks in Phoenix.

resolved. They will never photograph or display the burials, as the Zuni are now using this as a sacred area. They have also built a museum at the site to curate the retrieved artifacts and, despite being in an isolated area, there were 60,000 visitors last year. This intrigued our hosts and there were lots of questions about the site and about the preservation techniques.[11]

We then were shepherded into a large room where TV crews were set up. As we mulled about talking to the various staff members who had small displays of their materials set up, the video cameras churned. Dr. Masson and Shereen talked for a while about the Institute and about the delegation and then the session broke up as we divided into the various departments (I also met A. Kaspazov, a palaeozoologist who knows Richard Meadow[12] and C. C. Lamberg-Karlovsky). I went to the Palaeolithic department and heard Dr. N. D. Praslov[13] talk about the Kostienki sites, which date to about 40-20,000 B.P. They are multicomponent and are believed to be settlements associated with nearby kill sites (the latter have not been found). He discussed in detail, through the translation of Dr. Timofeev Vladimir I. (Head of the Neolithic group),[14] the finds at the Kostienki I site, which dates to about 23,000 B.P. Here there were a line of hearths with a ring of artifact clusters surrounding this line which ran down the middle. They found distinctive arrow points, clumps of clay that might be part of an oven top (I suggested they might be balls actually designed for baking by heating them up first—something we find in the Eastern Woodlands), a bone point stuck in a mammoth bone, and very realistic figures of stone and antler. There is a lower layer at this same site that dates to 38,000 B.P. Dr. Praslov also said that they have found a bison kill site, a jump of some sort, which dates to 22,000 B.P., so that would be the earliest in the world that I know of.

---

11 John W. Hohmann, Diane E. White, and Christopher D. Adams, "Architectural Variability at the Site of Casa Malpais, Arizona." Poster presented at the 58th Annual Meeting of the Society for American Archaeology, St. Louis, MO, April 1993. https://www.yumpu.com/en/document/view/6839984/shpo-old-library-document-arizona-state-university Library Number, SHPO Project Number 4648-R, SHPO-1993-0173.

12 Dr. Richard H. Meadow is Director of the Zooarchaeology Laboratory at the Peabody Museum of Archaeology and Ethnology, Senior-Lecturer on Anthropology at Harvard, and Project Director of HARP—the Harappa Archaeological Research Project.

13 Dr. Praslov was the Head of the Department of Palaeolithic at the Institute for the History of Material Culture, St. Petersburg.

14 Dr. Vladimir I. was a senior researcher in the Palaeolithic Department, Institute for the History of Material Culture, St. Petersburg.

Figure 8.
(Left) Delegates confer with Russian archaeologists at the Institute for the History of Material Culture.

Figure 9.
(Below left) A display of Scythian artifacts at the Institute.

Figure 10.
(Below) Kostienki I site plan, showing hearths relative to houses, circa 21,000 B.C.

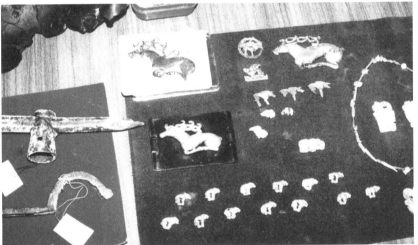

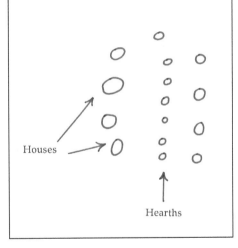

We next heard a talk about the Kokorevo and Kurtak complexes by one of the staff members. Both are later temporally than the Kostienki sites. The Kokorevo have microblade cores, points in mammoth bone (the mammoth had healed) and microblades that are still set within the bone points. The Kurtak complex has large unifacial blades but lacks the microblades, and the bone points have no insets.

We all distributed cards, gave various reprints to each other, and then had a formal session in Dr. Masson's office, which felt like a political treaty signing. Dr. Masson gave various papers to Shereen and talked about his hopes for future cooperative arrangements as the rest of us sat in a circle around them.

We then had a marvelous meal at a seafood restaurant followed by dividing up into three groups. Most people went to the Hermitage. Some went to the Military Museum at the fortress, and a small group went to the Ethnography Museum, now known as the Peter the Great Museum of Anthropology and Ethnography. I went there, as I wanted to see their Indian collections. Messages were mixed up though and apparently, they had expected us earlier. Our guide who was extremely friendly and very fluent was Girenko Nikolay. We were not able to get a card from him, but he should be thanked for his hospitality. Not so the Director Dr. Albert K. Baiburin who was very gruff and had a distinct military nature. We were definitely invading his turf. He sat there smoking and skulking at his large desk. A strong, muscular man with a sneer. Periodically he would stand at the window and blow out smoke. Also, as Nikolay was talking in English, at profound points he would nod his head slightly, so he knew what was going on but was unwilling to engage. This was the arrogance of a superior position.

Nikolay took us down to one of the Ethnography offices, talked to us some more, and then handed me over to someone who took me to the North American exhibitions. The room was laid out like the old Hall of the North American Indian at the Peabody, even with the same cases. Each culture area was isolated and cases within the areas were devoted to specific tribal groups.

Figure 11.
Meals provided the delegates were out of this world, which contrasts with what the typical Russian citizen was eating.

Figure 12.
Artifacts at the Peter the Great Museum are crammed into cases. The 18th-century geometric-style Chilkat blanket (probably Tlingit or Tsimshian Indian) shown here was nailed to the wall and folded to fit the case. It is one of the rarest objects of its kind in the world.

Figure 13.
Tlingit warrior diorama in the Peter the Great Museum.

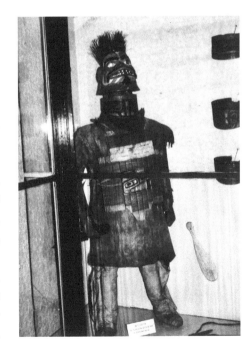

As would be expected, the Arctic and Northwest Coast were represented best. I spent quite a bit of time photographing many of the objects and their display procedures. Some of the full-size dioramas were fairly well-done, but the cases themselves hid them. Not being able to read the labels put me at a disadvantage, so I should not be so critical. They could use some conservation assistance though, as indicated by one example, their precious 18th-century Chilkat blanket in geometric style. This and the "Swift Blanket" from the Peabody are two of the three (I believe) that exist in the world, and yet it hangs by nails from the wall and is all bunched up in order to get it in the case. I suggested to Shereen a future delegation of museum conservators who could offer some advice on basic inexpensive conservation. This might be something People to People could consider for the future.

The museum also had a central display that was the original collection of Peter the Great. It consisted largely of pickled babies with bodily deformities, as well as two-headed calves, various Siamese twins, and the skeleton of a "giant." He must have been around 6 feet 7 inches! Wouldn't Peter be surprised today by American basketball. They would at least receive a central place of honor in his holdings.

After leaving the Peter the Great Museum, we took a long walk over the bridge and along the shore to three boats. Our group coalesced there from the three different museums and we headed off up and down the Neva River and into the canals. I sat on the upper deck behind the driver and quickly learned to lower my head as we floated beneath the multitude of bridges. This pleasant trip provided a much different perspective of St. Petersburg and it definitely was a highlight.

I got to talking with one of our guides Albert Yakimovsky. At one point he asked me if the scientists in my delegation are religious. I said that I don't know and that he must remember that I have known them for only one day longer than I have known him, and that these things are seldom discussed right away. I then said that I myself believe very much in God, but that I don't believe in organized religion, at least for myself. He explained how it was always expected that scientists in his country would be atheists or they couldn't be scientists. He himself used to be an atheist, but he is a believer now. We then talked about death (burial patterns), martyrs and saviors, and the comparative importance of Tolstoy vs. Dostoevsky. He was definitely not a fan of the former and said it was even difficult to obtain a Russian edition of Tolstoy's works because they are seldom in print. I was amazed at this. Pushkin seems to be much more the hero. As the sun set in the distance and we gently paddled along the river, I found a friend and confidant in Russia. Another barrier was broken.

Figure 14.
The author enjoying the canal tour.

Today we journeyed to Staraya Ladoga, a Russian medieval town east of St. Petersburg. The site is located on the left (west) bank of the Volhov River and consists of a fortress, currently undergoing excavation, and an associated town which is still very much occupied by a village. To get to the village one travels for about two hours along Rt. 18. Along this route you meet military trucks (converted for other uses?) and regular trucks, but very few cars. The people of St. Petersburg seldom travel outside the city limits. You will not find young people hiking, backpacking, or cycling, and people do not go out for a "spin" in the country. It just is not done. But there are people there, just behind the tree line in what appear to be run-down villages. And behind the trees themselves there are signs of occupation. On one of our two rest-stops I strayed from the bus and discovered the sunken foundation of what must have been an old house. Several others occurred nearby and in the middle of the one nearest me were signs of recent usage. A fire hearth, a seat, broken glass, and an excavation in the sides of the foundation with a makeshift toilet apparatus indicated a rustic abode. I wondered if I was being watched.

Dr. Natvienska gave us a tour of Old Ladoga. It used to be called just Ladoga, but when Peter the Great established New Ladoga, this town received its current appellation. Our initial reception took place right outside the Great Tower at what would have been the landing at the old harbor of Ladoga Lake. The water was now distant from the fortress and lower because of glacial rebound. Excavations began at the site in the early 18th century, commissioned by Peter the Great, so there have been three centuries of excavations there. The site itself appears in the chronicles by 806, but from dendrochronology they know it started by at least 753, so it is somewhat older than Kiev and Novgorod, which are of ninth century date. Old Ladoga was on the Byzantine route. It was a major trade center and its population consisted of Slavic tribes, Baltics, Finns, Vikings, etc. All written chronicles of the period are connected with this town. The Ruriks were here as was Oleg. He went to Kiev in the 880s and shifted the capital there, but he maintained important connections with Old Ladoga.

The fortress that is visible at the site now dates back to the late 15th–early 16th centuries. But this was not the first fortress. Excavations have revealed an

Visit to Staraya Ladoga, a medieval town.

The countryside.

Lunch atop burial mounds.

Banquet in St. Petersburg.

Figure 15.
Late 15-century
reconstructed
fortifications at
Old Ladoga.

earlier one (outlined by stepping-stones that cut through the middle of the open area), which is much earlier. It was, in fact, the first stone fortress in eastern Europe. There were two churches erected in the middle of the fortress. The first one, a wooden one that is recreated now, was built in the ninth century possibly, but at least by the middle of the 10th century. The later church, known as St. George, was of stone and was built in A.D. 1165 to commemorate victory over the Swedes. The present fortress, which has been undergoing restoration since the 1970s, is relatively small, but it does have five towers connected by stone ramparts. I took a series of photos of the group standing on the "Secret Tower," called such because of the secret passageway from the fort to the river. Two additional towers were currently being excavated, but they were so exposed that I wondered how they fare in the winter. Here again, some conservation/preservation advice might be useful.[15]

I walked along the bridge into town and checked out their large-scale excavations for finding earlier fortifications (lots of rich black earth, an indication

---

15 For a later and more detailed discussion and interpretation of the early medieval fortifications at Ladoga, see Nikolai I. Petrov, "Ladoga, Ryurik's Stronghold, and Novgorod: Fortifications and Power in Early Medieval Russia," in *East Central and Eastern Europe in the Early Middle Ages*, ed. Florin Curta (Ann Arbor: The University of Michigan Press, 2005), 121-27.

Figure 16.
The excavated tower shows stabilization methods.

Figure 17.
Within the fortress walls is St. George Cathedral, built circa A.D. 1165.

Figure 18.
A picnic lunch atop one of the kurgans north of Old Ladoga on the Volhov River.

of much earth movement) and I could see the mounds of midden all around the town, but thus far the emphasis has only been on the fortress.

We had our lunch north of town, again on the left bank of the river. We ate near Oleg's grave, the subject of a Pushkin poem. A prophet named Volhvic, whom Oleg once encountered, predicted his death. The prophecy was that he was to die by his horse, so to prevent this from coming true, he had his favorite steed killed. When visiting the grave of this animal two years later, a snake emerged from the ground and bit him, thus fulfilling the prophecy. His grave was somewhere within the multitude of conical mounds in the park we attended. These mounds were about 4 m. tall and relatively steep cones. I counted at least five of them and the one I ate atop had an enormous cavity in it, the result of an 18th-century dig according to one of our guides. The mounds themselves were constructed in the eighth-10th centuries and were a continuation of the earlier pagan beliefs. Very little were deposited in them, excavations having yielded only a few human bones, some charcoal, and minimal (if any) artifacts. This is why they have stood unmolested, for the most part, for so long.

On the way back we stopped at a store to do some souvenir shopping and then we returned to the hotel to prepare for the banquet. We each donned our best outfits and met at the bus around 6:30 p.m. to go to some restaurant. Our Russian guests were already there and had been there for quite some time. Once again, communication is a big problem in this country. When we first went in all of us were in shock. There were at least 50 of us, but only about four tables and sitting room for no more than 20. Plus, it was not a sit-down meal, but a banquet of nicely prepared (but not enough) food on a central table. What had the potential for disaster turned out to be a great success. People milled about the table making connections and were not confined by seating arrangements. It turned out much more pleasant that way, and most of the Americans ate lightly so that our Russian guests could eat as much as they liked. We knew that this was a great bounty for many, if not all, of them. I met and talked with Dr. Shetenko A. Ja., who is an archaeologist specializing in Pakistan, Turkmenia, India, etc.[16] He knew C. C. Lamberg-Karlovsky and Philip Kohl[17] (who he

---

16 Dr. Shetenko was also employed by the Institute for the History of Material Culture History, St. Petersburg.

17 Dr. Philip L. Kohl is Professor Emeritus of Anthropology and the Kathryn Wasserman Davis Professor Emeritus of Slavic Studies at Wellesley College.

looks like), so that made a firm connection with him. He complimented me at one point. When he found out I was 41 and not 30 he was astonished. He stood back, looked at me and said, "You must be a body builder." He was to get my best gift! The arrangement of the banquet also provided for ease of toasting and there was much of that. Everyone joined in with no prompting at all, and there were many very emotional toasts. I talked about the last three days and how my personal feeling varied from coldness and depression to warmth and a love for their city and people. I then mentioned my long talk with Albert on the boat and agreed with the previous Russian toast-maker that we are all related.

Some of the delegation returned by subway, but I decided to go by bus as I still needed to pick up some film at the store and I wanted to get things packed (or at least most of them) before the morning. With that done I took a hot bath and settled down with *The Cossacks*. Despite Albert, I am glad for Tolstoy's words.

WE HAD A FULL DAY OF TOURING TODAY. DOWN TO BREAKFAST AT 8:30 A.M. Again, everything starts late in Russia, or at least in St. Petersburg. People do not get rolling right away. It is usual for lunch to be after 2 p.m. and for dinner it is not unusual to be eating at 8 or 9 p.m. Businesses do not seem to be open until 9-9:30 a.m. Somehow, I expected everybody to be up and at it by 6 a.m. However, I should note that in our rides through the country people were still in their gardens uprooting potatoes at 8 p.m.

Immediately after breakfast we brought down our bags to the lobby. I then bought a small toy plane for Cabot, some stamps for postcards, and a collection of stamps as a gift. We drove through town to the art market which, at 10 a.m., was just beginning to open. We were the first bait. I ended up buying an original watercolor of the St. Peter/Paul Cathedral, an icon for Nancy, and two homemade dolls for Cabot and Avery.[18] It was difficult to get by any stall as each of the merchants (often the artists themselves) were over-anxious and often insistent that you bid on their products. Once again, the bulk of the material consisted of lacquer boxes, nested effigies, scarfs, military medals, painted eggs, and dolls. Somewhere in St. Petersburg there must be a warehouse of these things, as well as hats, postcards, and stamps, because they are all that are offered on the streets.

After increasing my suitcase weight accordingly, I got back on the bus and we all drove to St. Isaac's Cathedral. This structure is imposing on the outside by its massiveness, but it looks more like a City Hall in the States rather than a cathedral. As a result, it is difficult to anticipate what is on the inside. The beauty is absolutely overwhelming. We were not allowed to take pictures and my words certainly do not do justice to the magnitude and elegance of the art. There is very little in the way of stained glass in the cathedral, which is why it does not really look as such from the outside, but stained glass, in general, is not characteristic of Russian Orthodox churches. Instead there are gigantic mosaics and paintings of various images (Jesus, Mary, St. Isaac, St. Nicholas, etc.), which circle around and around the interior. What is most magnificent is the multicolored marble

---

18 William Cabot Brown, my son, was just shy of five years old when I was in Russia and Avery Lambert Brown, my daughter, was nine.

from Russia and Italy that forms the surface of everything it seems, and the gold gilt is everywhere, and done to such extraordinary skill that it never had to be regilded. The cathedral itself can hold 4,000 people standing up, which gives a sense of its size. It is the fourth tallest cupola structure in the world at 101.5 m. and it is also one of the largest cathedrals in overall size. When it was first built in 1710 it was made of wood and was constructed close to the Neva River. This one sank so a second one was made of stone in 1768 farther from the banks. The Tsar thought this was ugly so a third was constructed, but this was not liked either, so for the fourth one a competition was held. The Frenchman, Montferrand,[19] came up with a design which won, and though he was excellent at design, he was not so practical when it came to engineering. The weight of the structure resulted in its sinking. As a result, they had to place hundreds of wooden piles beneath the stone. These design problems added many years to the construction and so it was not until 1858, 40 years later, that it was completed. There had been a prophecy that Montferrand would live to see it in its final state

Figure 19.
A scene along the canal.

Figure 20.
The art market in St. Petersburg.

19 Auguste de Montferrand (1786–1858).

Figure 21.
Street signs reveal a mix of
Russian and English.

Figure 22.
Church of the Resurrection, where
Alexander II was assassinated in 1881.

Figure 23.
A renovation project. Note the rather crude
scaffolding on the right.

Figure 24.
One of the Rostral Columns located at the forks of the Neva River. It commemorates ships that were sunk in naval battles.

Figure 25.
The Winter Palace is one component of the Hermitage Museum.

Figure 26.
Stairway within the Winter Palace leading to exhibits.

Figure 27.
A royal room.

Figure 28.
The lady guards are diligent in their roles.

and he did indeed die only several weeks afterwards. Upon his death, it was understood that he would be buried beneath the cathedral that he had invested so much of his life in making, but that was not to be. Because Montferrand was a Catholic, the Tsar felt it would not be right to bury him in a Russian Orthodox cathedral, so his body went back to France.

We also drove by and took pictures of the Church of the Resurrection which our guide, Alona Tchistyanova, referred to as the Cathedral of Sacred Savior on Blood. Construction began on it in

1881 to commemorate the murder of Alexander II who was assassinated on that spot in that year. We finished up the tour in the Hermitage, which, in this case we concentrated on the Winter Palace (only one of the many buildings). It is an absolutely marvelous palace, remarkable as much for its architecture and decor, as for its treasures within. Alona took most of the people on a tour, but as I was trying to see the Scythian material I drifted off from the rest.

Unfortunately the Scythian gallery was closed, so I toured alone. Spent most of my time looking at the

Figure 29.
The Alexander Column and General Staff Building, as viewed from the Hermitage.

paintings but did join up with Albert and Joel (Grossman)[20] and learned something about the former function of many of the rooms. Eventually my goal was to get out of the building, as we had to meet the bus at 2:30 p.m. and I wanted to at least stand in the square ground at the Alexander Column where the Revolution began. Getting out of the Winter Palace was no easy feat though. One room filtered into the next and although there was a proliferation of directional arrows for exiting, I never seemed to make much headway in finding the true egress. I almost found myself trotting through the treasures at one point in trying to get out.

I shouldn't have worried because the bus was nowhere in sight when I emerged. Several of our group were clustered in the center of the plaza and from a distance they seemed to be swatting at flies. The flies turned out to be Gypsies of varying sizes and shapes—mostly mothers and children. They offered no wares, but had begging down to an art. They are poverty incarnate, wearing rags and dirt as their clothing, and they give one no respite in their begging. With one hand you clutch your back pocket and with the other your camera and you desperately try to avoid contact as they cluster around you. Usually they have their first finger

---

20   In 1992 Dr. Grossman was an archaeologist and President of Grossman and Associates, a cultural resources management firm in New York City.

pointed upward as they beg. It is disheartening to see the women with obviously undernourished babies on their backs, and they follow you as you twist and turn trying to literally get in your face. At one point they all disappeared only to coalesce as a group beneath the Alexander Column where, what appeared to be, a major confab went on. I don't know whether they were counting their earnings or planning their next strategy, but it certainly looked ominous. Also in the Square were bears on leashes. They rolled and playfully performed for their masters who also were looking for funding. And of course the other hawkers were there with their medals, postcards, and sketching abilities (that was a new twist). I did buy a beach hat... an appropriate gift for Rick.[21]

We finally departed St. Petersburg after having had lunch at the same restaurant that we were at last night and headed toward Novgorod. The ride was nice. Very flat land, usually with extensive fields on either side. Giant apartment buildings hovered in the distance while strings of run-down houses bordered the road. Each gable-shaped abode had a garden, complete with apple trees and associated outbuildings. With the exception of two ornate houses that we stopped at, these houses were by no means picturesque. There is great poverty in this country and whether you are in the country or city it is all around you. To some children at one of the houses I traded rubles for the little flowers they picked for me. They seemed pleased and I pressed the flowers in the book I was reading.

Finally we are in Novgorod where we are staying at the Hotel Intourist. It is nicer than I expected. We ate next to a band and near an unruly batch of young military men celebrating some great event. The crashing of goblets against the wall suggested some happiness.

One thing I neglected to mention was a "rest stop" we visited. There were two little chalet outhouses, which no one dared to enter. As is usual in this country, things are erected but not maintained. I'm sure they have never been cleared out. Most of us headed into the woods to do our business. Also at this rest stop was the equivalent of a Seven-Eleven, a little open-air stand of beverages and foods. A brazier was alit with pork shish-ka-bob sizzling. Behind it were a couple of stools if you wished to partake. Some did, but most took in the scene and protected their bellies. You just never know.

---

21 Richard S. Fuller was my colleague with the Gulf Coast Survey at the Alabama Museum of Natural History at the time. See Ian W. Brown, *Richard S. Fuller, Southeastern Archaeologist: Warts and All* (New Orleans: University Press of the South, 2020).

I CANNOT BELIEVE THAT I VOLUNTEERED TO BE RECORDER FOR TODAY. THIS HAS HAD to be the most difficult day in terms of the diverse things we did and the complexity of the names and events. However, I'll give it a go first in my journal and, subsequently, in the summary account for People to People's purposes.

After a hearty breakfast at the hotel we started off the day by driving to the Novgorod kremlin, the fortress in the center of the city. Our guides were three archaeologists from St. Petersburg: Olga Scheglova, Oleg Boguslavsky, and Alexey Plokhov who is of the Novgorod Expedition. Once in the kremlin we divided into two groups. I went with Olga and Alona (as translator).

Novgorod: history of the kremlin and town.

St. Sophia Cathedral.

Chamber of Facets.

Museum in the Administrative Chamber Building.

Lunch at the Detinets.

Church of the Transfiguration.

Museum at the Gate Tower excavations.

Evening service at St. Sophia Cathedral.

The kremlin, the inner fortress of the town, is of relatively recent date (15th century). Kremlin is a Greek word that was first used in Russia in the 14th century, and it means, basically, the sheltered part of the town, that which must be protected, like a mother protects a child. Novgorod, however, has a much longer history. It is located on the Volhov River far upriver from Old Ladoga, which we visited two days ago. As Old Ladoga was situated by the lake of that name, Novgorod was placed in the vicinity of Lake Ilmen. Currently Novgorod is a city of about 250,000 but before WWII there were only about 40,000 people in the area.

Novgorod itself means "New Town" and, together with Old Ladoga, they were the two great communities along the Volhov. They figured strongly in trade connections north and south. According to the chronicles, Novgorod is supposed to have first been occupied in the mid-ninth century, but thus far archaeology has only been able to detect mid-10th century settlement. The Ruriks were the first to settle the area. As I understand it Oleg, the son of Rurik, was a Scandinavian prince. In 862, the same year he captured Kiev, he also began the community of Novgorod. These were Baltic people, not Slavs. The first settlement is believed to have been in the Urlevo area. Novgorod has always been a two-part city, divided in half by the river. The west bank is known as the Sophia part of town, after the cathedral, and the east bank is called the Market part of town. Two large monasteries mark the limits of the town, one on the north near our hotel, and the other on the south known as Urlevo. This settlement moved to the Sophia area in the mid-10th century. According to Dr. Khoroshev, who spoke to us later, there were three different centers of Novgorod that coalesced at this time. This action marked the beginning of the Russian state. In the 10th and 11th centuries Kiev and Novgorod were of equal status, as state power shifted back and forth between the two. But of the two Novgorod was the first state capital.

Novgorod started as a pagan state. As Natalia Solodkova told us later, it did not become Christian, in part, until 959. The monastery Urlevo was the first sacred place for Slavs, and pagans and Christians lived side-by-side.

After discussing the history of the early settlement, we moved back into the kremlin from the gate overlooking the river and viewed the bells of Novgorod. The ones that are exhibited there now were constructed in the 17th and 18th centuries and are meant only to symbolize Novgorodian independence. The story is that the large bell of Novgorod was used in early times to call the people together. Once congregated, they discussed things democratically, like whether or not to go to war, whether to invite princes into town, etc. They were very proud of their independence. Ivan the Terrible, however, targeted Novgorod as he desired their wealth, and in 1570 he killed more than 2,000 of their inhab-

Figure 30.
Bells are symbolic of
Novgorod independence.

itants to obtain it. In the process he carted away their giant bell, but it was too heavy. Therefore, he had it destroyed and broken into many pieces in the town of Valdai. According to legend, each of the pieces was made into smaller bells and hung in the churches of Valdai, a sign of Novgorod's independence and freedom.

Olga then told us of the St. Sophia Cathedral and its history. Apparently, Prince Vladimir I (or Vladimir the Holy) brought Christianity to Russia. He had 300 wives but couldn't marry one woman who he really desired because he was a pagan. Therefore, he converted to a Christian and made his people in Kiev change in 988. Novgorodians did not want to change, but the town fell to Christianity in 990. Vladimir's son began construction of St. Sophia in 1045 and it was completed five years later. It stands at 38 m. tall and is another symbol of Novgorod. The cupola of the cathedral once served as a lighthouse, a beacon to the city. The cathedral itself was built by artisans from Kiev who were paid for their services. They were not forced to build it. In 1570, when Ivan the Terrible was ravaging the town, a pigeon is supposed to have landed on the cupola and turned to stone, which is why one sits there today. The cathedral was partially

Figure 31.
St. Sophia Cathedral within Novgorod's kremlin is a majestic edifice. It was built circa A.D. 1050.

destroyed during WWII, but it is the original structure. It is amazing that when Novgorod was finally taken by the Nazis in WWII there were only three dozen people left in the city. According to Natalia Solodkova, the city was captured only twice—once by the Swedes in the 17th century and last by the Germans.

Olga told us about the monument in the center of the kremlin. It was erected in 1862 in the shape of a bell, a symbol of the city. On it are represented the images of all the heroes in Russian history, in military, literature, music, etc. Pushkin, for example, was very visible for his African features. I asked if he had been subjected to prejudice, because of his race. Olga seemed surprised by the question, and said "Prejudice yes, but because of his highly politicized poems, not his color." This monument was pulverized during the war. Only a single figure survived, but it was all rejoined and repaired.

Novgorod stands out as unique because of luck or ability to have remained independent. When the Mongol invasion took place in the 1230s-40s, all the rest of Russia was destroyed. Novgorod was recognized to be a rich medieval town, so they had every intention of devastating it. An army advanced on Novgorod in 1238, but when they came to a crossroads, they took the wrong route and missed the town entirely. It is for this reason that there is so much standing architecture of the pre-13th century. The chronicles also were preserved, as was the culture itself. The documents at Novgorod are distinct also in that they deal with the common folk, whereas the Kiev chronicles focus primarily on the elite. The reason for this has much to do with the pagan religion, which was so common at Novgorod and that was more communal in orientation. The pagan religion in this part of Russia was named after the Volhov River and was called Volhvic. This was also the name of the pagan priest. As regards architecture, that of the kremlin walls (15th century) is quite similar to Moscovite construction, showing influences from that direction. Originally there were 31 towers defending the kremlin.

When Olga finished her tour, we joined up with Natalia Solodkova. She originally was an architectural specialist on the staff, but with cutbacks in jobs the only way she could stay on was as a museum guide. This job situation is so dismal in Russia. One of the boys who was hawking postcards to us on the streets said that his father was some sort of a scientist, but as he makes only about $30 a month it is not enough to support his family. As a result, the boy quit school because in one day's time he can make far more than his father can in a month. How can this situation benefit the country?

Figure 32.
The Facet's Chamber was the archbishop's residence in 1570 when Ivan the Terrible used it for his infamous banquet. The building survived World War II.

Figure 33.
A fresco within the Facet's Chamber dating to the 16th century.

The first stop on Solodkova's tour was the Facet's Chamber, or Chamber of Facets. This was the Archbishop's residence in 1570 when Ivan the Terrible killed him and massacred most of Novgorod's inhabitants. This was also the location where Ivan the Terrible held his famous banquet. Although 90% of the buildings in Novgorod were destroyed or badly damaged during WWII, this structure was the only one to survive the war intact. The archaeological collections and icons were taken to Germany. The icons eventually came back, but the archaeological artifacts never did. The first exhibition opened in the Facet's Chamber in 1959. It was like looking at the crown jewels in this one small gallery. They were displayed nicely with solid security and some decent conservation measures. Humidity gauges are used quite frequently in the Novgorod exhibits, in marked contrast to the practices at St. Petersburg.

We next went to the Administrative Chamber Building where we learned about their extraordinary collection of icons. This building was destroyed during the war and, as stated, the icons were taken to Germany. Over 7,000 icons were taken and although 300 came back, not all were returned to Novgorod. Many ended up in St. Petersburg much to the chagrin of the Novgorodians. The reason for so many icons has to do with the number of churches. Between the 11th and 16th centuries, 160 churches were built in the Novgorod area and just before the Revolution, 54 of them were operative. All of those that we saw in the Administrative Chamber Building came from those churches and they are the ecclesiastical symbols of Novgorod. The collection that we saw was the third largest in Russia. All of the painted ones came from the Novgorod area and were produced between the 11th and 15th centuries. The first signed one was made in 1294. The oldest icons from St. Sophia's Cathedral consisted of three rectangular slabs, each with four panels to a block. These date to 1341. We also learned that the metallic cover of the icon protected the important painting beneath it from the candle tallow and, at the same time, it also shielded it symbolically. It is clear from the quality and quantity of icon production, that Novgorod played a critical role in the cultural history of Russia in terms of religion.

We took a break from the museum and ate lunch at the Detinets, which is the city's best restaurant. It is situated within the kremlin's walls and formerly was a prison for females during the second half of the 19th century, primarily for whores and thieves. In most of Russia male prisoners were put in monasteries and females in nunneries. The Detinets is a fascinating structure. To get to the dining area you ascend a "double-lane" complex, spiral stairway all made

Figure 34.
The Detinets Restaurant,
a 19th-century prison for
women and the scene of our
heavenly meal.

Figure 35.
The "double helix," a spiral
stairway in the Detinets
Restaurant.

of wood. Like a corkscrew it shoots straight up, and then you must duck your heads and walk up through a dark passage to an open hall. In the dining area you sit at long wooden tables in matching crude clumsy chairs, apparently the same ones used by the prisoners. We ate our beet soup (semi-borscht) with lacquer spoons and then had a meat & onion stew. The desserts consisted of a pancake soaked with hot honey, followed by ice cream made of what appeared to be goat's milk. All in all, it was a fine dining experience.

We then returned to the Administrative Chamber Building to see the archaeological collections. We each paid our 50 rubles to permit our use of cameras and, in this case, flashes. We could not use flashes in either the Facet's Chambers or when viewing the icons. The archaeological exhibition is arranged chronologically starting with medieval Novgorod and continuing through to present times. There was a large section on the Soviet era, appropriately all in red. I had the impression that Solodkova was not particularly interested in showing us anything after the 16th century. The materials were exhibited far better here than anything we had seen at St. Petersburg, but they were helped enormously by the quality of the artifacts themselves. What makes Novgorod so unique archaeologically, of course, is the preservation of its organic objects due to anaerobic conditions. The objects got wet immediately and stayed wet.

Plus there is great variety. You not only see the finished products, but the tools used in producing them. Novgorod clearly was a great manufacturing and trading area. In fact, the first coins in Russia were made in Novgorod. We saw those, the birchbark letters for which Novgorod is famous (730 found), and many other artifacts.

We then left the kremlin and walked over the river to the Market part of town. There Natalia took us to the Church of the Transfiguration. It has a much larger name, but I was not able to record that. This small church was built in 1374. It is small in terms of floor space, but quite tall and was a major investment in time and money—but they were all over the place, wherever we looked. The Cathedral of the Virgin of the Sign, for example, fronted immediately on the Transfiguration Church. Natalia said such churches would have supported about 20-30 people, so only a few families. A local wealthy man would commission it, thus purchasing his way to heaven, and the families who used it would continue to invest their life savings in it throughout their lives. There are marvelous frescoes in the Church of the Transfiguration, and we saw the best of them in a small chamber that we got to by mounting a tight stone-paved stairway in the back of the church to the second "floor" (more an aisle). The frescoes were painted in 1380 and what makes this church so unique is that the painter is known.[22] All of the churches in Novgorod had painted frescoes, including St. Sophia, because they could not afford marble. This particular church had had much restoration in the 1920s and the frescoes were in superb shape, even though they had been affected by fire many times, but there was great destruction to it in WWII and restoration continues today.

Natalia left and we were joined by Dr. Alexander S. Khoroshev, one of the heads of the historical division of Moscow University and the excavation head's right-hand man.[23] He took us to a museum located at the Gate Tower excavations.

---

22   Theophanes the Greek (c. 1340–c. 1410).

23   Dr. Khoroshev's formal title was Deputy Director of Novgorod Archaeological Expedition.

Figure 36.
The Church of the Transfiguration was
constructed circa A.D. 1374.

Figure 37.
(Below) An example of a small Russian Orthodox
church within the kremlin in Novgorod.

The collections housed there were from all over the city and were nicely displayed on two floors. The excavation background (methods, history, crew photos, etc.) was on the first floor and the artifacts on the second. Work started in Novgorod in the late 19th century, but major investigations did not begin until 1932. Moscow University had just celebrated its 16th year (1976) of continuous field schools in the city.[24] As stated earlier, Novgorod was originally made up of three different centers along the river that eventually combined as one. Medieval Novgorod was 99% made of wood, which was perfect in archaeological terms because of the wet soil conditions, the anaerobic environment resulting in the preservation of items that, in turn, has made Novgorod one of the finest museums in the world for such materials. Fire also contributed to our knowledge because there was a major conflagration about every 40 years. When that happened, new construction began atop the previous. We saw pictures of roads and buildings stacked on top of each other. In all, there were 28 distinct building stages between the 10th and 15th

---

24   An excellent summary of archaeological work at Novgorod, up to the time of our trip, is Valentin L. Yanin, "The Archaeology of Novgorod," *Scientific American* 262, no. 2 (February 1990): 84-91.

centuries. Because of the rich quantity of wood as building material, archaeologists in Novgorod made heavy use of dendrochronological methods. They have been able to get within a five-year accuracy level for such dating. As a result of their rich collection of diverse artifacts, typological studies have progressed also, and they are able to date contexts within a 15-year accuracy level by relative dating procedures.

Birchbark letters were undoubtedly the most exciting and profound discoveries at Novgorod. The first one was found in 1950 and there are now 745 recorded, 15 more than mentioned by Natalia. Their importance comes not from revealing the literacy level of these medieval folk, but in connecting the archaeological excavations with what is known from the history (the chronicles).

The artifacts are truly amazing. Especially intriguing are the carved hands grasping various cylindrical objects. They could be part of larger effigies or they might be phallic images. They date to the 11th-12th centuries. All of the wood is beautifully preserved. When it first comes out of the ground they keep it in water, but then they use a sugar solution with the sugar gradually taking the place of the water so that the object maintains its shape and stability. It seems to work great and there is no evidence of a plastic-like coating. It is similar, apparently, to the jam-making process. The wooden objects of the 11th-13th centuries were elaborately decorated. This is because objects were made to order from skilled artisans. Afterwards decoration started to diminish, as objects were being mass produced.

I was amazed to see tiny *Flushloop* bells dating from the middle of the 10th to the middle of the 15th centuries. They lack circumferential grooves and have large thin wire loops for handles.[25] Toys consist of wooden animals on wheels, much like what one will see in stores today, as well as chess, checkers, dice, stuffed leather balls, etc.

We got back to the hotel at 6 p.m. and I began my marathon journal writing for the day. I had intended to remain at the hotel and finish it up, but would have felt so stupid not going to the Russian Orthodox service at St. Sophia. This was a religious holiday, marking the transition from summer to fall. The priests were performing service all night, but the public could remain only until about 9:30 p.m. Only about eight of us went, guided by Olga and Igor. The women had to

---

25 Ian W. Brown, "Trade Bells," in *Tunica Treasure*, by Jeffrey P. Brain, Papers of the Peabody Museum of Archaeology and Ethnology 71 (Cambridge: Harvard University, 1979), 197-205.

wear a skirt and tie a scarf around their hair. The men, however, could not wear anything on their heads and had to keep their hands out of their pockets. We walked on the dark streets to the cathedral and when we got to the side door the priests and all the congregation were marching out. The candlelight procession, complete with choir, slowly passed us and I felt like I was witnessing a scene from the Middle Ages. Behind the religious persons in a tight cluster were the elderly ladies. Each of them had the same shape, varying from 5 to 5.5 feet in height with huge bottoms and small rounded shoulders. All were crag-faced with no attractive visages. Each of them scurried forth around the edges of the procession trying desperately to be as close to the line and to the priest as they could. While the mass of humanity encircled the cathedral we went inside and prepared for their return. Each of us respectfully found a position along the wall or in other obscure locations so that we would intrude as little as possible. But to no avail. The priest and his company took up shop right in the center of the floor and a giant circle of worshippers clustered around. Whether or not we liked or intended, we were part of the ceremony. We all felt particularly awkward when bodies fell to the right and left of us as worshippers knelt and prayed. This happened repeatedly and continuously throughout the service and I felt like I was playing dodge ball trying to stay to the side. I did not want to be conspicuous and ruin their ceremony, but they seemed to be oblivious to our presence. Each of them was anointed by the priest upon leaving the church. Igor gave me a medal of St. Nicholas, which I shall give to Avery.

I went back to the hotel and continued to write my journal until 11 p.m. Read some more in *The Cossacks* and then set my clock back because of Daylight Savings Time...

HAPPILY I WAS NOT THE OFFICIAL RECORDER TODAY, SO I DIDN'T HAVE TO FEEL guilty about not always hovering close to our guides. However, I did take a lot of notes, so I do have considerable writing to do. After breakfast we drove to the southwest corner of the city near the statue of Alexander Nevsky, the defender of Novgorod. Here we visited the Trinity Site, named after a church that used to be close to the dig. Dr. Khoroshev guided us around the excavations. They had finished by the beginning of September, but everything was still exposed. Water covered most of the deep pit and when they excavate what they do is dig small pits and trenches so that the water seeps into them. Then they drain it by pumping it out, leaving the soil dry by the time they start digging. Khoroshev estimates that they drain about 1.2 m. a year. They are now quite deep in their work (looks to be at least 3 m.) and are on the border of the 11th-12th centuries.

The Trinity site is the main scientific site they are investigating, but there are always other small excavations going on. This past summer they were testing four other areas in the city. It was clear in the excavations where structures and fence lines were located. Next to it was the backdirt, which also had scattered throughout it leather patches, potsherds, glass, bone, etc. Khoroshev said we could take whatever we like from it because it was out of context, so I secured a small collection of about five items...[26]

We next visited the excavation that Moscow University has been conducting in the kremlin's walls. This cross-section through the wall is occurring at the small tower located just south of number 10 on my map.[27] The current walls of the kremlin date to the 1490s. A kremlin existed earlier in the 11th-13th centuries, but it was made of timber rather than brick. The earlier fortifications, made of oak, were dismantled and formed the foundation for the stone walls. For many years sinking problems have resulted in great cracks in the walls and in 1991 this part of the wall collapsed. Their investigations were designed to find out the reasons why and how construction actually occurred. The timbers that

---

26 These materials were donated to Harvard's Peabody Museum, Deed of Gift 1/12/95.

27 A map was given to us, which I made marks on as we toured the excavations. It is not repro-
duced in this work.

Figure 38.
Alexander S. Khoroshev and delegates at the Trinity site.

Figure 39.
Waterlogged deposits show fence lines and house outlines. The current excavation is at the 11th-12th century level.

Figure 40.
Close-up of the building supports and fence lines at the Trinity site.

Figure 41.
Details on how the wooden paths and fences were constructed, as seen in a diorama at the Administrative Chamber Building.

Figure 42.
(Bottom left) The backdirt is not screened and it often contains artifacts.

Figure 43.
Strip of leather from a 11th-12th century object recovered in the backdirt.

they found were stacked in neat symmetrical rows with clay packed all around them to keep them from shifting. The clay, basically sterile of artifacts, was recovered from the moat, so the moat clearly had been operable in the 11th-13th centuries. The timbers formed the embankment and then bricks were set above it. The core of the fortification is a thick stone rubble with a brick facade. Giant arches form the basic structure to support on the ramparts a 2-m-wide platform. There were great exposures available for photography. The reason why the walls keep cracking is that beneath the timber embankment are 2 m. of cultural strata that are very spongy. This is clearly a problem that is not resolvable.

Figure 44.
(Far left) One of the kremlin's towers near the excavations. Note the giant arches for support, as well as the wide platform on the ramparts.

Figure 45.
Construction of the 15th-century fortifications at Novgorod. A brick facade hides a thick layer of stone rubble.

Figure 46.
The interior wall of the kremlin is to the right. The Detinets restaurant, the scene of our wonderful meal, occurs in the background.

Figure 47.
A trench through the kremlin's fortifications. The timber walls date to the 11th-13th centuries. They were then neatly stacked and used as a base for the brick and rubble walls erected in the 1490s. Clay was excavated from the moat and packed around the logs to keep them from shifting.

Figure 48.
The weight of the stone fortification depressed the underlying soil and wood foundation.

Natalia Solodkova took over as guide when we drove to the Yuriev Monastery. On the way we saw some wonderful recent cemeteries with each family plot surrounded by iron fencing gaily painted in blue. Unfortunately, we were not able to stop to get pictures. The Yuriev Cathedral translates as St. George Cathedral. It has onion-shaped cupolas, which replaced dome-shaped ones in this portion of Russia in the second half of the 17th century. Supposedly, this is because the onion shape was much better adapted to the heavy snows of the Russian environment. The height and size of the Yuriev Cathedral allowed for incredible acoustics. Services in this structure must have been grand. Yuriev once had the third largest number of icons in Novgorod. This church was unusual also in that it and only one other in Novgorod had tombs within the church. They were exposed to our view, the burials having long since been disturbed in searches for wealth. The two burials located to the left of the door upon entering were past mayors. A bishop, perhaps two, once rested at the door, and there were also cysts for two young sons of a prince. They died around 1190, possibly from having been poisoned. The wall painting was done at the end of the 19th century by the same people who painted St. Sophia Cathedral.

Figure 49.
Beach in front of the Yuriev Monastery, Novgorod.

Figure 50.
*The Yuriev Monastery and Cathedral. This translates as the St.
George Cathedral.*

Figure 51.
*Vendors selling their
wares outside the
monastery and
cathedral grounds.*

Figure 52.
Delegates gather at the entrance to the Yuriev Monastery and Cathedral.

Figure 53.
Interior of the Yuriev Monastery. Russians have a great love for flowers.

Figure 54.

The Yuriev Cathedral has onion-shaped cupolas, which replaced dome-shaped ones in the late 17th century. This cathedral once had the third largest number of icons in Novgorod and has wonderful acoustics.

Figure 55.
Examples of the frescos within the Yuriev Cathedral.

Figure 56.
A painting in the interior of the Yuriev Cathedral cupola.

Figure 57.
Entrance sign to the Vitoslavlitsy Museum of Wooden Architecture in Novgorod. Churches and houses were moved here from all parts of the region.

We next visited the Vitoslavlitsy Museum of Wooden Architecture, an open-air museum of houses that had been moved from various parts of the Novgorod area to one location. Most have been restored to some extent, but much of the original houses are preserved. The first house we went into dates to the 1870s. After going in another house, there is a clear pattern to the layout. The overall shape is a steep gable structure, very large and with a roof that slopes steeply, almost to the ground. A large workshop area (cooperage) occurs on the second floor, which is the main living and working area. This is because these houses were built along riverbanks and flooding often occurred. There is an open space adjacent to the stairs that overlooks the sleigh parking area, and another open space next to the workspace that overlooks the domesticated animals, reasonably snug for the winter. The living quarters occur in the front of the house with a general living and sleeping area to the left. Children would have slept in a loft. During the day,

Figure 58.
This is a typical house of the 1870s. Despite its size, there is actually very little living space in the structure. Most of the house is used for livestock and workshops.

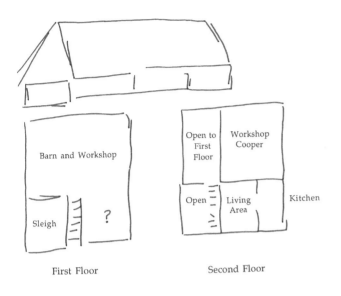

Barn and Workshop

Sleigh ?

First Floor

Open to First Floor | Workshop Cooper

Open | Living Area | Kitchen

Second Floor

Figure 59.
A schematic drawing of the house in Figure 58.

Figure 60.
A kitchen in the same house.

Figure 61.
The second-floor workshop,
also in the same house.

Figure 62.
Two large wooden churches on the grounds. The Church of Peredki (1599) is on the left and the Octagonal Church (1757) is on the right.

the loft would have served as a storage area for items not in use. Adults slept on the floor. To the right is a small kitchen area. Clearly, the bulk of the house was designed for critters and working.

The very large church that I photographed dates to 1599. The other large church, the one with the octagonal walls, dates to 1757. Neither of these could we enter.

If this outdoor museum is characteristic of the type, they are very formal and sterile. The houses, as artifacts, are superb and of great interest, but this is by no means a living museum. There was a woman weaving on a small loom in one of the domestic houses, but otherwise these women, like those in the other museums, are merely guards. They are not there for interpretation, their role largely being to thrust your flash down your throat if you try to take pictures. And what was annoying was that permission varied from house to house! I was not one to mess with these women, however. There are gardens behind the various houses, but no live animals or any activities associated with farming. These gardens are for show alone.

I was interested in the construction of the houses, particularly with regard to joints. They made heavy use of the double saddle joint, squared ones, and unique ones like that used for the Octagonal Church. I took pictures of all of these.

Figure 63.
A close-up view of the unusual joints of the Octagonal Church.

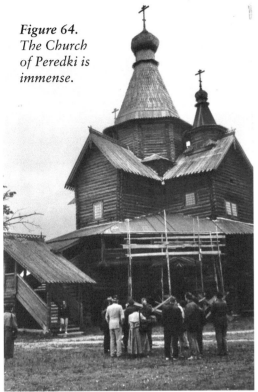

Figure 64.
The Church
of Peredki is
immense.

Figure 65.
To the right of the Church of Peredki is the Peasant Cottage of Izba.

Figure 66.
(Bottom left) The Peasant Cottage has double saddle joints.

Figure 67.
Another church at the
Vitoslavlitsy Museum.

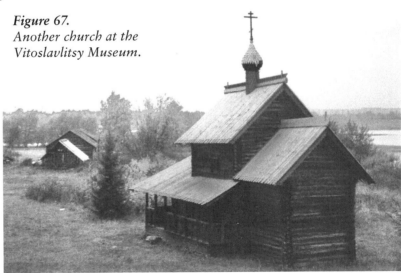

Figure 68.
Another highly decorative church on the grounds.

Figure 69.
(Above) The church in Figure 68 has squared joints and a railing with geometric cutouts.

Figure 70.
The only "living" parts of the Vitoslavlitsy Museum are its gardens.

Figure 71.
Children of any time
seem to enjoy swings.

We returned to the hotel for lunch, rested a short while, and then went to the Museum of Musical Instruments where we were treated to a wonderful lecture and concert of instruments based on the pieces found in the Novgorod excavations. I did not obtain the name of the restorer, but he was accompanied by five ladies dressed in mid-19th century Slavic costume from the Moscow area. They were the traditional dancers for his music. The museum is in the process of construction, and they are relying heavily on gifts from private individuals both within and outside of Russia. They also receive a little from the State. This week they are having a conference on the material in commemoration of 60 years of excavations at Novgorod (the major excavations I assume). He showed us and played many of the instruments, which included two kinds of bells, one attached to clothing and another to the necks of cattle so they won't get lost, ceramic rattles that were tied to cradles to keep evil spirits away from the children, various other rattles of wood, and lots of string instruments including a miniature cello which he played for us with a bow made of the bough of a tree. He also played a flat board as a drum. This was used by shepherds. Jews harps were also played. Only five have been found at Novgorod, but they occur in layers as early as the 14th century. He also showed us small wooden flutes that are short, but thick.

Figure 72.
The Museum of Musical Instruments had only recently been established when we visited Novgorod.

They were used to accompany dancers, so they specialized in repetition. The bows used horsehair, while strings were made out of the intestines of rams. This information they have from ethnographic data. There are three strings on these small instruments, one is melodic and the other two are drones.

There are also harps that have five strings, so they make only five sounds, and a lyre-like instrument known as a gusle. The early ones have a large hole at one end of the narrow sound board. Instruments of this type were common in Europe in the first millennium A.D. and from the Novgorod finds it is clear they were used in Eastern Europe too. An important difference, however, is that the Western European ones have a bridge that can be moved. The more recent gusles at Novgorod lack the large openings. Fir and pine were the most common woods used in manufacturing these instruments, but oak was used also. Between the 12th and the 20th centuries the holeless ones were used. More strings were added (now eight) and the instrument was laid horizontally with both hands coming down on the string board and neck. Previously the left hand went through the hole and the instrument was used like a guitar. The fingers of the left hand plucked the strings while the right hand strummed. This was done in the 11th-century gusle form. For the later ones, the right hand would continue to strum but the fingers of the left hand were arranged between the strings and were used to soften the sounds.

The music that all of these instruments produced was eerie and, naturally, medieval. These instruments were used in ensembles as early as the 11th century, and probably earlier. Children learned by direct instruction from their parents. Music would be taught until they were about seven years old and then children would basically be on their own. Only men played instruments, while both men and women sang and danced. For the music that they played for our group, they used ethnographic material and "the old way of tuning," whatever that is.

Detailed notes on the six bells that I observed in their exhibition: Two are of the Lapped Edge type and of these one is a definite *Clarksdale* bell. The other is very small and with an enormous strap. There is also a very large bell with a wide equatorial seam that is probably crimped, but is certainly well-smoothed. It has a very thick loop. The bell metal for this specimen is quite thick and at first I thought it was cast brass, but it is not. A fourth bell has two intersecting slits in its base and the bell bulges out at the termination of each slit. The top of this bell comes to a peak and there is a small wire loop on top—altogether unusual. There is one small *Flushloop* bell like those seen at the Gate Tower museum yesterday and another bell that looks silver. It looks like a *Flushloop* bell but is not. It is very deformed.[28]

After this exhausting day we went back to the hotel and had 45 minutes to do some packing and prepare for the banquet to commemorate our stay in Novgorod. All of our guides and translators came, and the banquet was once again a standup affair. The music/dance people also came. I was sad to say good-bye to Alona, as I will miss both her translating and her pleasant company. She was a real delight. I gave her a box of three fragrant soaps and an invitation to visit my family if she ever comes to the U.S. After eating and a series of toasts, I left the festivities early as I had some serious writing to do. I am very grateful that I am in a single room because I'm afraid that had I been with someone else it might have been quite difficult to maintain a record of this trip in a form that I can use. Went to bed a little after 11 p.m.—have to be up at 4 a.m!

---

28   For a description of the various bell types and varieties, see Brown "Trade Bells," 197-205.

From Novgorod to the
St. Petersburg airport.

Flight above the steppes.

Mineralnye Vodye and
the Northern Caucasus.

Russian hosts.

AS I SIT HERE ON THE MORNING OF THE 29TH, AS I WRITE, I AM OVERLOOKING THE snow-capped domes of the Northern Caucasus Mountains of Essentuky. Having just finished *The Cossacks*, it has a special meaning. We are in the Sanitorium Moskva (Resort Moscow) and I am in Room 402, a single suite with a balcony and even a chandelier. This hotel is the meeting/resting place of the former Soviet Union dignitaries, so the rooms are quite elegant. Our standards are definitely changing though. Just as I now am concerned with the value of a dollar and what I can obtain for it, I now look at the room I am in as elegant. In the States it would be considered a dingy, low-maintained cheap room, and the hotel as well. The mind starts to shift, even over the course of a few days.

We got up this Monday morning at 4 a.m. and left Novgorod an hour later. We each had a bag of sustenance, which included strawberry-flavored mineral water, coarse bread, cheese, and slices of pressed ham meat. I could not stomach this so early, so I did not start to consume anything until we reached the St. Petersburg airport, and even then I could handle only the cheese, bread, and drink. I cannot get used to having their meats in the morning, or at any time for that matter.

We left all of our bags in the bus for fear of items being stolen (Paul has had that experience every time he has been in this airport) and we just walked around or sat around while waiting for check in. Mostly we just tried to shake out the cobwebs. The ride to the airport went through much of the same countryside, which once again consisted of ramshackle house units along the road, vast fields of cabbages primarily, and major apartment complexes in the distance. I guess the road houses were permitted to remain because they did not interfere with the extensive farms.

The airport was small and unclean, with horrible smells emanating from the restrooms in the basement. Security was minimal but I don't think I've ever heard of anyone hijacking a Soviet aircraft. It was easy to get on to the tarmac if anyone so desired and the administrative building looked almost as if it was bombed out. I suppose it was sheets of aluminum foil that adorned the windows, but from a distance it looked like laundry. Our plane was excellent, considering the reports I had had about Aeroflot. It was a giant aircraft which sat about 400. Once again, we herded into the cattle car to be taxied to it and we then ascended into the belly of the plane. There we deposited our carry-ons and learned that the definition of "carry-on" also included such things as bicycles and tires. The flight was smooth and uneventful, just the way I like it. We could not see much because of the clouds, but when patches of ground did come into sight the unusual land system of the steppes was apparent. There was no order to the positioning of the land plots. They just seem to fan out in whatever shape and size evolved through time. It is a surveyor's nightmare. Clearly, the Soviets just adopted what already existed, rather than resurveying all the land into uniform sections. The people reside in small communities occurring at regular intervals and in the vicinity of adequate water. The rivers near each community often are dammed, presumably for both water and hydroelectric power. I doubt that recreational purposes were considered in their construction. The large apartment buildings, omnipresent in the north, are lacking or minimal in the portion of the steppes I observed from the air. The house units, or at least what I could make out of them, once again had a disheveled appearance. Part of the reasons for this has to do with low maintenance—once something is built it either has to stand of its own accord or fall—but also I believe it is related to a process of house construction. Houses do not appear to be built at once; rather, they evolve. Sometimes one sees only the shell of a house. As it is weathered, it appears to have been abandoned, yet it is merely awaiting its next stage—walls and windows. Once they are in, the residents take up quarters—so then one starts to see some curtains and perhaps an outer coating of some material to insulate the house. Now it looks like a shack. And on and on until the house is finished. If the rubles do not come in, the houses may not obtain the latter stages of their evolution, which is why everything always seems so tattered and worn. But again, there is minimal litter. This has much to do with the cultural tendencies of the Russian people, I am told, but I'm sure it is also related to the social conditions—times are so tough that nothing is wasted. Bottles, cans, paper, aluminum foil, plastic, etc. never reach the dump. Somewhere, somehow there will be a use for these items in a land of extreme shortage.

We arrived at Mineralnye Vody in the Northern Caucasus in the mid-afternoon, and then had about a 45-minute ride through the countryside. This land is very beautiful, but the Soviets clearly never let beauty get in the way of progress. Each of the isolated hills in this region are scarred by intensive mining. Often only a stump remains of the original rise. We continued to ascend in altitude above the steppes until arriving at our destination, the Resort Moscow Hotel.

Figure 73.
The Resort Moscow
Hotel is considered to be
one of the finest hotels in
the country.

Figure 74.
A market located near
the hotel.

Once again, we went through the routine of waiting for keys and lugging our bags, but none of this was aggravating. We are a very loose group (archaeologists as travelers usually are) and I have heard few complaints.

After getting settled, we had our dinner (I have to get used to saying dinner rather than lunch because this is our major meal) at 3 p.m. and then rested until 6 p.m. We then met with our professional guides and contacts for this last leg of our journey. Most of these people came down from Moscow and seem very excited to have us there. We are the first delegation of U.S. archaeologists to have traveled and toured the sites in this part of their country. It seems the farther we travel from St. Petersburg, the more expected we are, the better we are received, and the more planned the activities. Somehow I had expected the opposite. Not that St. Petersburg was bad, by no means, but things seemed so much more formal and political there, especially when the various directors were around.

Figure 75.
This area is the mineral water capital of Russia and is a great retreat for those who vacation. Summer homes in the mountains are quite common.

Our principal host (non-academic) in Kislovodsk is Alexander Vardanyanz, the "Poisk" ("Search") sponsor. He gave the greetings, as did Sherry, and then Dr. Sergei Kullanda[29] spoke. He introduced the four or five others, his colleagues, and then spoke for a few minutes. We then learned what our exciting tour will be, including a couple of days of helicopter rides to sites. During the break I

29   Dr. Kullanda was with the Institute of Oriental Studies of the Russian Academy of Sciences in Moscow.

talked with a Sergei Korenevsky[30] and we then had a short talk on the cultural history of the region by Prof. Vera Kovalevskaya,[31] with Kullanda translating. She talked about the Palaeolithic sequence and its similarities with that found in southern Europe, extending from the Pyrenees to the Levant to the Northern Caucasus. In Mesolithic times the same caves were used that had been employed by Upper Palaeolithic people. By the Neolithic, strong influences came in from the Near East, but by the Early Bronze age at around the 4th millennium B.C. contact with steppes populations is very evident. The chariot was borrowed from the Near East and the horse from the Pontic steppes, so all the greatest inventions came together in the Northern Caucasus. There is so much ethnic diversity in the Caucasus. Kullanda referred to it as, "The Mountain of Languages and the Mountain of Nations." We talked a lot about the problems of language correlating with material culture in the U.S. and they agreed they had the same difficulties here the farther back in time they proceed. After the discussion, we ourselves proceeded to supper and then retired early for the evening. I took a nice, hot long bath and finished reading *The Cossacks*.

---

30 Dr. Korenevsky was a Scientific Advisor at the Institute of Archaeology RAS, Stavropol Museum.

31 Prof. Kovalevskaya was with the Institute of Archaeology in Moscow.

AS I DISCOVERED THIS MORNING, AND CORRECTED ON YESTERDAY'S ENTRY, WE ARE in Essentuky, not Kislovodsk. These two towns are part of a conglomeration of four towns that form the resort area population of about .5 million. In driving through these towns you could feel that they are very different from what we had seen earlier. The houses are older and quainter, but still not well-maintained. Most have fences around them, to keep various livestock in more than to keep people out, and the yards are cluttered with various outbuildings. Most of them also have a haystack plunked in the middle of the yard for animals to feed off in the future months. If there is a preference for color, I would have to say it is "baby blue," but even this is used sparingly as there must be a great scarcity of paint—or it is expensive.

We then drove due west of Kislovodsk along the banks of a river through country used for grazing cattle and sheep. Many stables were erected along the southern bank of this river, actually more like a large stream. In fact, it was through the erection of a stable complex and associated buildings that the Koban-Alan cemetery, the Klin-Yar site, was discovered. Andrew Belinski, who was there with his child and beautiful red-haired wife, introduced us to the archaeologist in charge, Yakov Berezin.[32] He had his crew digging frantically the last few days to show us two of the catacombs dating to the Koban-Alan culture. They had done an incredible amount of digging in such a short time, as my pictures hopefully show. They knew of the fortress on the hill for a long time because of the visible structures, but they were only alerted to the catacombs in 1987 when the foundation of a building hit one that yielded two full helmets of Assyrian type. The site dates to the Iron Age and early Middle Age. It is a huge burial site and odds are that no matter where they put a shovel they will eventually hit one. The Koban culture dates between the seventh-eighth centuries B.C. and burials relating to it are well represented in the stables area.

The catacombs date to the fourth century A.D. and relate to the Alan culture (or Alanian). These are not catacombs as they are usually considered—tombs

---

32 Dr. Andrew Belinski was the Chief of the Northern Caucasus Archaeological Expedition. Dr. Berezin was the Head of the Archaeology Department at the Kislovodsk Museum of Natural History.

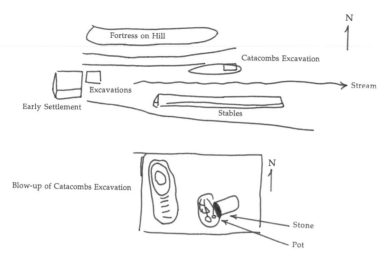

Figure 76.
Sketch of the Klin-Yar site, a Koban-Alan culture settlement and cemetery west of Kislovodsk.

Figure 77.
The Klin-Yar site of the Koban-Alanian culture is located in a very strategic position. The high foundation for the fortress appears in the middle distance to the left. This settlement was situated along the Great Silk Road.

in stone chambers—but they were dug in the ground. The tomb to the east on the accompanying drawing [Fig. 76] was relatively shallow, about 2 m. below the surface. A tunnel leads to it with a stone blocking the entrance to the grave. Shallow graves like this were of lesser status than deeper ones. This particular tomb was used only once, but others were returned to many times, so there existed open cavities for these. According to Yuri N. Litvinenko,[33] who I spoke with later, Late Scytho-Koban (fifth-fourth centuries B.C.) in the Stavropol Forest that were used repeatedly were the burial chambers of richer families. For the larger tomb, the one to the west, they had not yet hit bottom, but Berezin expected it would descend to about 5 m. below the present ground surface. He estimated that the present surface was only about 20 cm. above the one in the fourth century A.D., so these were deep excavations. Considering the narrowness of the trench I would have begun to worry about the safety of my crew about a meter ago. The bones have revealed evidence for tuberculosis and syphilis.

The actual settlement for this cemetery was located upstream in an area that had undergone heavy construction. Some test excavations were done in that area, but it is believed that most of the site is destroyed. These people were the direct descendants of the Samarts.

---

33 Dr. Litvinenko was the Head of the Archaeology Department at the Pedagogical Institute of Stavropol, in charge of science consultation and interpretation.

Figure 78.
The location of the catacombs excavation relative to the fortified settlement on top of the promontory.

Figure 79.
(Below) Delegates approach the Klin-Yar catacombs excavation. The tombs date to the Iron and early Middle Ages.

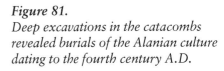

Figure 80.
(Below left) The smaller tomb located within the excavated area.

Figure 81.
Deep excavations in the catacombs revealed burials of the Alanian culture dating to the fourth century A.D.

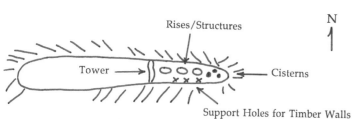

Rises/Structures

N

Tower

Cisterns

Support Holes for Timber Walls

Figure 82.
(Top left) A stone blocks the passageway to the burial chamber and the exposed skeleton. This particular tomb was used only once.

Figure 83.
(Top right) A very deep shaft led to the larger tomb, believed to be about 5 m. below the present surface.

Figure 84.
(Middle left) A more detailed sketch of the fortress at the Klin-Yar site, a medieval fortification of the Alanian culture.

Figure 85.
(Left) The cliff leading to the fortress was approachable in places, but it still would have been a major deterrent to invaders.

The fortress, a medieval fortification of the Alanian culture, dates from the sixth-ninth century A.D. The fortress occurred on a high isolated hilltop overlooking the catacombs area.

The inhabited area was on the eastern end where the people were defended by natural agencies on three sides and an artificial tower on the fourth. A large robber hole occurred in this embankment. There were timber walls along the south side (at least) as evidenced by support holes drilled into the limestone at regular intervals. Berezin gave me a piece of pottery from the site, which dates to the sixth-ninth centuries A.D.

We then traveled southwest of the site, about 5 km. to another fortress that was occupied at the same time and which, along with Klin-Yar and three other towns, was important in controlling the Silk Route through the Northern Caucasus. While walking to the site, Litvinenko explained that the earliest Scythian archaeological remains (eighth-seventh centuries B.C.) were located to the

Figure 86.
(Top) Delegates face east on this very narrow promontory, but it served its purpose as a fortress. It was of Alanian culture design and dated from the sixth-ninth centuries A.D.

Figure 87.
(Middle) This view along the fortified promontory is to the south. The road that can be seen to the right in the middle-distance wraps around the site.

Figure 88.
(Bottom) The current road has probably been situated in the same place for millennia as part of the Silk Road. The caves in the cliffs are still used to fence in livestock.

Figure 89.
Haystacks and livestock dot the landscape of the ancient Alanians.

Figure 90.
Site of the fortress overlooking Honey Water Falls.

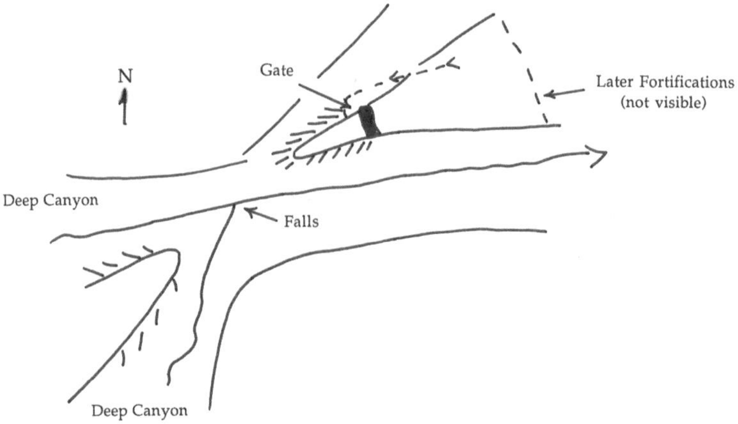

Figure 91.
Sketch of the Alanian fortress at Honey Water Falls.

east, from the Black Sea in the Northern Caucasus, and further up to South Siberia (Arzhan).

We parked the bus and walked over the fields to the Honey Water Falls site,[34] a name I surely can remember. On the way we passed dozens of kurgans, or burial mounds. As there was no farming in this area in recent times, none of the kurgans were destroyed. As a result, they have been able to plot the location of all these mounds quite accurately. For each of the five towns, the living areas associated with the mounds covered about 100 acres and each was fortified to some extent. The Honey Water Falls site was just a fortress. There was no associated settlement site. All of the fortresses were in view with at least one other, so they could communicate with each other quite rapidly. The Honey Water Falls fortress was protected by a solid stone wall that was about 4 m. wide and 4-5 m. tall. There were no gates in this wall because the entrance was made by a fissure in the limestone cliff off the northern side of the enclosure. Anyone entering the area would have to turn sideways coming up this fissure and would be unable

Figure 92.
The only access to the interior of the fortifications was a narrow fissure in the rock.

34   This is also referred to as the Ukazatel site.

to use arms or defend himself. There were no cisterns in this fortification and the lack of a large living area, associated structures outside, or easy access to the top, suggest that there was only a small residential population at the site initially and that its purpose was more for communication. However, by the 11th century A.D. the fortress wall had extended east for quite some distance, almost to where our bus was parked, so there was an appreciable population there then.

We stopped at the falls for a rest and to view it. While there I spoke with Janet Pollak[35] who recommended that I read *A Hero of Our Time* by Mikhail Lermontov, as it deals with Cossacks.[36] Once people had ambled back up the

Figure 93.
View of Honey Water Falls from the fortified site.

35 In 1992 Dr. Pollak was Associate Professor of Anthropology at William Paterson College in Wayne, New Jersey.

36 Mikhail Lermontov, *A Hero of Our Time,* translated from the Russian by Vladimir Nabokov in collaboration with Dmitri Nabokov (Ann Arbor: Ardis, 1988).

hill, we drove to a nearby restaurant called the Love and Treason Castle. It was built in 1936 and commemorates a story about two lovers who decided to plunge to their death. The man jumped first, but the woman thought otherwise and declined to follow. Hence the name. In such circumstances I recommend holding hands. We then proceeded to have one of the finest meals of my life, one that received a hearty clap from all of us at the end. We started off with an exotic salad of carrots cut into flower shapes, stuffed slices of bell pepper, stuffed and pickled eggplant and a por-

Figure 94.
(Left) The Love and Treason Castle.

Figure 95.
((Far left) The cliffs above the castle, scene of the treachery.

Figure 96.
(Below) The restaurant at the Love and Treason Castle was reported to have the finest meals in southern Russia—we all agreed.

tion of a chicken dish. Then came the soup, which was extremely hot (thermally and chemically) lamb stew. This was followed by broiled trout and home fries, the finale being homemade ice cream and dates. It was incredible.

When we finally finished the meal we rolled out of the restaurant. We all gathered in various groups and tallied for a while. We then followed Dr. Korenevsky who led us to a picturesque, but very noisy, spot along a stream. He brought artifacts and arranged them along the ground. He then proceeded to tell us about the history of the area from Neolithic times to the Mongolian invasion. I do not have detailed notes on his lecture, but I will at least transcribe what I did take notes on. What we really need is a chronology chart that plots the names and general dates, because it's very difficult to stay with the talks. I figure that after two more days of this we will at least be able to talk intelligently about it.

Some of my notes: The forest in the Caucasus is on the north side of the mountains. Not coincidentally, the production industries began in the Northern Caucasus in the Neolithic when the forest first appeared. Obsidian comes from the Central Caucasus and the production of tools/quarries, etc. is related to Armenian production. They use this industry as a temporal marker in the Caucasus as well as in the Ukraine and Romania. They should be able to connect it with the Ubaid period in the Near East.

Kurgans in the Central Caucasus mainly cover the graves of military men and rulers. They include weapons and silver/gold jewelry. For certain cultures it is not known what women's jewelry looks like.

The Alanian period begins after the early Iron Age and continues up to the Mongol/Tatar invasion. They destroyed the population, took the wealth, and left, so the area was abandoned thereafter. However, between the Neolithic and the 12th-13th centuries A.D. there was strong continuity in the area.

We called it quits as the sun was setting and headed home. As we are to have an early day tomorrow, I immediately sat down to writing—I knew I would not have time in the morning. I skipped the main part of dinner, but did partake of salad, dessert, champagne, and tea. Returned to my room to finish note taking, to take a bath, and to begin *The Don Flows Home to the Sea* by Mikhail Sholokhov.[37]

---

37 Mikhail Sholokhov, *The Don Flows Home to the Sea*, translated from the Russian by Stephen Garry (New York: Vintage Books, 1966).

Nancy's 40th birthday today. I tried to send her a Telex, but when I found it was going to cost in the range of $30-$60, I thought otherwise. I hope she knows I am thinking of her. For $60 she would have been thinking of me, and I'm afraid the thoughts would not be pure.

What an exhausting day we had, yet so exciting in all that we saw and did. As I sit here at 6 a.m. on Thursday morning I am seriously contemplating skipping breakfast to transcribe my notes. I know that I will always get another meal, and for this trip, it will be grand, but I'm not so sure I will have any more time to sit back and reflect upon what we've done. And the worse thing for me is to have to confront pages and pages of chicken scratch and try to decipher their meaning. It will be difficult enough as it is.

Got up at 6 a.m. on Wednesday morning, had breakfast, and then caught the bus to the helicopter pads. Fortunately, we had a driver because the local airport that we used is certainly not recognizable as such. Like everything we saw, the buildings were decrepit and the landscape unkempt. We thought the buildings were uninhabited until the doors shoved open. The bathrooms were indeed inhabited, but with what organisms no one was able to identify.

We divided into two groups, half going into the white helicopter and the other half, including me, into the red. I had never been on a helicopter before, so I thought the increasing crescendo of the turbines as we attempted to become airborne was all in order. The wide-eyed stares of most other passengers with fingers in their ears suggested otherwise. We finally soared upwards and headed north and west out of the mountain range and into the steppes.

Before proceeding to the first site, I should quickly relate the chronology. I had asked Sherry yesterday if we could get such a chart and she received a handwritten one, which I quickly took notes on. After the various Paleolithic and Neolithic cultures came the Maikop culture. This is of Early Bronze Age date, with calendrical dates from the very late fourth millennium B.C. through all of the third millennium B.C. up to the beginning of the second millennium B.C. During most of the second millennium B.C. there were several Steppe and Local cultures in the area. This was the time of the Middle Bronze Age and Transitional Period. Then came the Koban culture which is Late Bronze Age to

September 30, 1992 (Wednesday)

Touring by helicopter.

More on culture history.

Burial mounds at the Vorovskolesskoe settlement.

Scythian life.

Excavations at the Razdolnoje site, a Scythian burial mound.

The Tatar site near Stavropol.

Stavropol Museum of Local History.

Figure 97.
Transportation in the
Northern Caucasus was
by military helicopters.

Early Iron Age, approximately 1300-700 B.C. As I am estimating the absolute dates from the chart, they might be off a little from dates I had recorded earlier. In such cases I would trust more the dates that I had actually heard from professionals' mouths. The Scythians are an Early Iron Age culture also, which resided in the area between 800 and 400 B.C., and they were followed by another Early Iron Age culture, the Samartians, between around 400 B.C. and A.D. 1. Then came the Alanians and Khazars, which were Early Iron Age to Early Middle Age peoples, A.D. 1–approx. 1200). Apparently, they do not use Middle and Late Iron Ages as period names in this area. The Golden Horde is this term for the occupations between the 12-14th centuries A.D. (the Late Middle Age), and I presume this refers to the Tatar invasion. Finally, the last occupation from the 14th century on are the Early Adygs, also a Late Middle Age culture.

The first site that we visited is called the Vorovskolesskoe settlement.[38] Our guide there was Vladimira Petrenko. We planted our copters in the vicinity of a

---

38 Vorovskolesskoe means "Forest-stealing village" (Yuri N. Litvinenko, personal communication, 1992)."

large mound, about 10 m. tall, which dates to the Maikop culture, according to Petrenko. This kurgan had not been excavated, but I assume we stopped at it because of its impressive size and so that Petrenko could provide background on the construction and usages of such tumuli. As we looked across the landscape we could detect dozens of other kurgans. She said there were over 100 in the locale. Work has been ongoing since 1973.

In the 1st millennium B.C. a stabilization of nomads occurred on the steppes. This was the time of the Scythians and was a period when military groups were established for both the protection of cattle and the acquisition of territory. Several kurgans in this area are of seventh century B.C. date and excavation of them revealed several layers of social status in the society. About 100 km. from the settlement that we stood on a royal burial was found in the center of one such kurgan. Retainers were buried around the edges of it. Nomads did not settle, so there were no established settlements near the burial sites, but these sites were a focus of their lives because they also served as temples. The Scythians had a cult of ancestors, which was closely associated with hero worship and the worship of their God of Sword, whom Herodotus identified with the Greek God Ares.

Both wood and stone were used in the construction of these kurgans. Wooden structures were erected both below and above the ground. A pit would be dug in the ground, above which a wooden structure was built that replicated the form of their tents. Social status rather than tribal association controlled the shape, size and physical arrangement of the components of such burial sites. Riding horses were buried with important individuals, as were silk clothes, jewelry, food for

Figure 98.
(Top) Aerial view of a kurgan in the steppes, the Vorovskolesskoe settlement.

Figure 99.
The Vorovskolesskoe kurgan, as seen from the ground.

Figure 100.
(Top) Vladimira Petrenko lectures on the Vorovskolesskoe settlement. It consists of dozens of kurgans dating to the Maikop culture of five to four thousand years ago.

Figure 101.
(Middle) From the top of one of the kurgans two others can be seen in the middle distance.

Figure 102.
(Bottom) Because of privatization, looting had become a major problem. The government could no longer give adequate protection to sites.

the dead in special jars, and pieces of the animals they ate. These were offerings to the dead. After the burial ritual a mourning feast occurred. This is known by the quantity of pits around the kurgans, which contain the remains of goat (considered a sacred animal), horse, etc. Goat heads are often found in such contexts, as well as postcranial remains. Also within the kurgans, in addition to the horse bodies, are found harnesses and parts to chariots.

Because none of the kurgans have been excavated in the area we landed, it is not known if they date to Maikop or Scythian times. In the Early Bronze Age (Maikop) kurgans housed only one burial, but by Middle Bronze Age times additional burials were made and the mounds often took on a hemispherical shape.

Next we went to the "nearby" (by helicopter that is) Razdolnoje site. Andrew Belinski was our guide there, as his students were busily excavating the site. In three weeks' time they had removed all of the earthen part of the mound and were down to the platform. As there were only about four of them, I would say they had moved some earth! Their tools were rudimentary, so this is an achievement, but there were no signs here or at any site we visited for sifting equipment, so that at least is one reason for the speed of their work.

This site is a Scythian barrow, which dates to the fourth-third centuries B.C. They selected it for excavation because it is analogous to ones that had been looted in the area. They originally started to dig it by excavating trenches in the north and south to determine its construction. At 20 cm. above the original ground level in the southern trench they started to hit stone. Heavy machinery was used to remove the overlying mound. At its base was a circular stone platform, which appeared to me to be raised about .5-1 m. above the ground. This platform lies above the burial chamber(s), so it is still not known what lies below. Two clusters of stones are visible on the side we studied (north), and these are probably the tops of the chambers. Belinski believes these chambers will have a tunnel emerging from the western side. I asked him whether they found

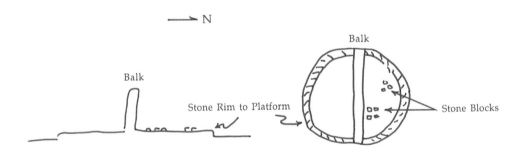

Figure 103.
Sketch of the Razdolnoje site, a Scythian burial mound dating to the fourth-third centuries B.C.

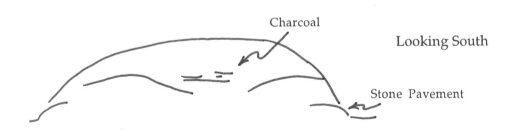

Figure 104.
Generalized section drawing of the Razdolnoje site burial mound.

Figure 105.
About half of the
overlying mound at the
Razdolnoje site had
been excavated.

Figure 106.
View of the east side
of the balk, showing
a certain amount of
complexity to the
mound construction.

Figure 107.
Andrew Belinski (left)
and Yuri N. Litvinenko
lecture on the site
excavations. A stone
ring on a raised platform
encircles the burial
chambers, which are
marked by clusters of
stones.

Figure 108.
Vladimira Petrenko
and Sergei Korenevsky
take a closer look at the
stratigraphy.

any burials in the earthen mound, but they did not here, and from the way he answered it sounded as if they seldom do. This was surprising to me, because he said that the platforms can be exposed from one to 50 years, so clearly there were family ties with the burial location. The platforms were used as temples, so does that mean then that when this function no longer applied, they literally "killed the temple" by burying it with earth? But that doesn't totally explain the complexity of the stratigraphy observed. Two arcs are clearly visible along the alternate edges, suggesting an earthen ring once encircled the mound. There were also considerable charcoal lenses, suggestive of ritual usage of the mound as it was being constructed. There is consider-

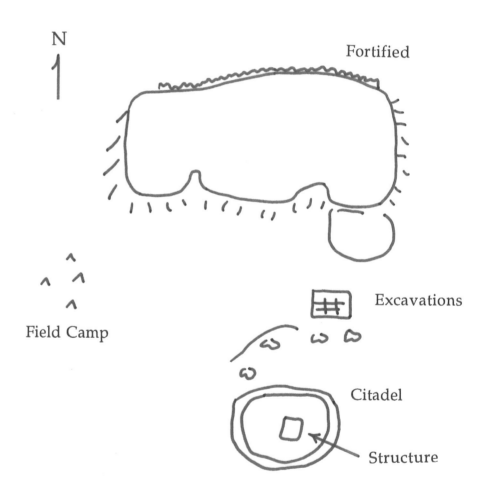

Figure 109.
Layout of the Tatar site in the Stavropol region, which dates from the Late Bronze Age to the 10th/11th centuries A.D.

able complexity in the mound itself, but I'm afraid it was just ripped out in anticipation of getting to the goodies below.

We were unable to spend much time at this site as we had so many things to do, so soon after the lecture we were herded back to the chopper. This was unfortunate as all of us wanted to walk around it seemed and breathe in some of the history of the region. We are moving too fast and it is starting to catch up on us as regards health (some are dropping out) and psyche—I heard the first murmurings of revolution today—glad I'm in the Red chopper.

We then flew to the Stavropol area, landing on an immense fortress site known locally as the Tatar site (much like "Spanish forts" in the Southeast U.S., all earthworks tend to be attributed to Tatars by the local population). Our guide to this site was the Director of the Stavropol Museum of Local History—Nikolai A. Okhonko. He had a contour map of the site which I photographed, but the basic layout of the upper portion is as depicted [Figure 109].

Okhonko first introduced himself and his museum. Stavropol, although a regional center with regard to archaeology, is important in that all excavations in the Northern Caucasus are done jointly with this institution. The Tatar site is the ancient capital of the area. It is the largest site in the central portion of the Northern Caucasus and it dates from the Late Bronze Age to the 10th/11th centuries A.D. It is naturally fortified on three sides and the north side was protected by artificial walls.

Okhonko then showed us the excavations currently underway in the southeast portion of the site. This was not the densest area of site occupation, but they dug there because elsewhere on the site there were squatters until recently. Once the site was declared a cultural monument they moved off. They hadn't lived in this location because it was so close to the walls of the citadel. Ten excavation units were open, and they looked to me to be either 4- or 5-m.-squares. There were two layers visible, but they had not yet got down to the bottom of the deposits. From the surface to the layer of white stones dates from the present back to the eighth-10th century A.D. Below that was the debris of Sarmatian occupation. They had found evidence for circular houses that were about 5 m. in diameter and made of timber and clay, but they do not have much settlement evidence as yet. The nomads would have lived in tents and as this settlement was on the boundary between settled tribes and nomads, a lot of the structures here would have left no visible evidence. This mixture is one of the major research interests of the scientists working here. In one portion of the excavations was a feature which is interpreted as a pottery kiln. We learned that the director of

Figure 110.
The gift. Joel Grossman received a rather hirsute coat in exchange for his "Indiana Jones hat."

these excavations was killed only several weeks ago in a horrible accident that occurred on the site. He had fallen out of a moving bus.

We then walked through the woods and into the citadel. There would have been no woods there at the time it was built and used, which would have been during the Middle Ages. It must have stood there earlier, however, because Okhonko said that it was so huge that even during the Sarmatian invasion in the fourth-third centuries B.C. they could not end its life, but this invasion did destroy many other monuments at the site. The citadel also survived the Huns' invasion. The best represented period for the site overall was between the sixth and eighth centuries A.D. Prior to the Sarmatians were the people of the Koban culture and they are believed to have mixed with the Sarmatians.

Back to the citadel. It was arranged in a circle having an approximate diameter of 100 m. There were two entries at opposing sides and they were designed so that it was difficult to gain entrance. They have not yet excavated the walls, but they were made of stone and it is clear from their present state that they must have been enormous. Okhonko also showed us one of the structures in the center of the citadel that was only half excavated. He believes that it might have been the temple. Its construction consists of large stones with small ones in between. It was at this point that he gave the Middle Ages date, so perhaps he was just referring to this structure rather than the citadel overall.

While in the citadel I talked with a young man named Yuri Gusev whose brother Vladimir recently had an article in Connoisseur magazine concerning the excavation of a Caucasus princess tomb. He thought his brother was famous and that I probably had heard of him.[39] Yuri stuck with me for the rest of the site tour and I found him to be a pleasant person to talk to. He enjoyed

39 I am ashamed to say I had not heard of his brother at the time. Vladimir Gusev, born in Moscow in 1957, is a very famous Russian painter (http://artrussia.ru/en/vladimir_gusev).

practicing his English and was quite fluent. At one point when we were at the fieldcamp we discussed families. I said I had two children and a wife and he said he had a wife and one child. But then his eyes lit up when he said he recently was allotted a new apartment that has two bedrooms, so they are planning on having another child. How different from the States. We think of having the child first and then change the accommodations, either moving to a bigger house or adding on a room, to satisfy the growing family. In Russia it seems that the accommodations are the first priority, the finite boundary, and family size is modified to suit it. Settlement patterns and their effect on society can be so dramatically different. How would we, as archaeologists, have been able to see these differences in attitude in the ground?

In leaving the Tatar site we mounted a wonderful air-conditioned bus, which had "poultry association" (in English) written on its side. Lord knows from where it came. Stavropol, we learned, means "City of the Cross." The city was founded by Catherine the Great in 1777 when the Caucasus was included as part of the expanding Russian empire. According to the usual story, when some foundations were being dug a cross was found, hence the name. Later I learned from Yuri Litvinenko that this object could very well have been planted by the invaders as ideological propaganda, thereby establishing a material linkage with Christianity on conquered territory. The main industry of the city and surrounding area is agriculture and the guides said that Stavropol is considered the "Bread Basket" of Russia." Considering that the Ukraine grows all the grains, however, "Fruit and Vegetable Basket" is probably a better appellation for Stavropol. And those they do have, as we learned in another wonderful dinner. Stavropol already has connections with the U.S. as she has a sister city—Des Moines, Iowa. Now that is grain country!

Figure 111.
A contour map of the enormous Tatar site was posted for our viewing.

Figure 112.
Facing south from the Tatar site toward
Stavropol. This site dates from the Late
Bronze Age to the 10th-11th centuries A.D.

Figure 113.
The entire field was within
the fortified area, which was
naturally fortified on three
sides. The north side had an
artificial wall.

Figure 114.
Nikolai A. Okhonko discusses the
excavations at the Tatar site. The
feature is believed to be the remains
of a pottery kiln.

Figure 115.
The archaeology fieldcamp at the Tatar site.

Figure 116.
Sergei Kullanda holds a pepper sauce bottle in the field kitchen. It's not quite Tabasco, but still rather tasty.

Figure 117.
Yuri Gusev with some of the artifacts from the Tatar site.

After dinner we attended the Stavropol Museum of Local History with Okhonko once again as our guide. He explained to us the significance of this region overall. Because it is north of the Kislovodosk region, Stavropol is at a lower elevation. Stavropol is located on both the north-south and east-west crossroads into the Northern Caucasus, thereby forming a bridge between the mountain groups and those of the steppes to the north. We then learned about the history of the museum and were given a tour of the archaeological gallery where we saw objects from tombs of the various cultures. We didn't have much time to focus on any one thing as we were moving so fast, but I did manage to take quite a few pictures, including pots of the Maikop culture showing con-

Figure 118.
Archaeological displays at the Stavropol Museum of Local History.

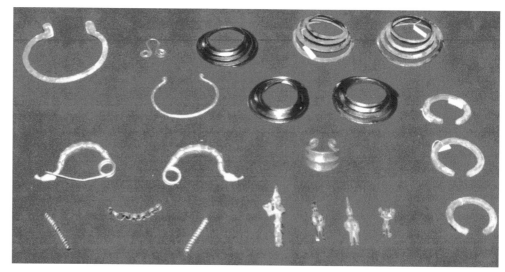

Figure 119.
A typical exhibit of Scythian jewelry.

nections with the Near East and various objects of the Bronze Age cultures of the Kislovodsk region. Seats had been set up for talks, but as we were running so far behind only Okhonko gave a speech. He talked mainly about what they were trying to do in the region in terms of archaeology, and he also expressed great concern and desired advice concerning conservation. The move to privatization is a bit disconcerting with regard to sites because they are now becoming private property. He also mentioned that it has just been in the last few years that they have started excavating more recent sites of the 18th and 19th centuries.

Figure 120.
A mammoth overlooks the natural history displays.

Outside the museum and behind it we viewed an Alanian stone tomb, which has various scenes along its exterior walls. The scenes are believed to depict the life of a ruler. One wall shows his life on earth, two in the nether world, and the fourth depicts heroic events. This monument had stood on top of the ground and the actual grave had been in the center beneath the surface.

Back in the helicopters and off to Kislovodsk. I never thought I would be able to sleep in a helicopter, but I kept nodding off, as did most others. In between I caught glimpses of the beautiful landscape dotted with kurgans, haystacks, flocks of sheep, and herds of cattle and horses. What a country! We drove back to the hotel. Igor, our guide, actually hitchhiked as he tried to get there earlier to pick up film from somewhere, unsuccessfully. Once back at the hotel, we only had a short time to get ready for supper. I ate very little as I was still stuffed from dinner. At 8 p.m. the Americans got settled in the conference room for an evening of papers, but the Russians did not arrive until 9 p.m. as their bus was delayed. Everyone (or most folk) went with the flow though. We then listened to six papers, supposed to be 10 minutes each, but more like 25, and crawled up to our rooms at midnight.

WE WERE ALL IN THE BUS AND READY TO GO AT 8 A.M. WHEN THE WORD CAME that the helicopters would not be ready until 9 a.m., so we went to the market near the hotel and did some souvenir shopping. I bought a couple of beautiful sweaters for 700 rubles each ($3.50), one for me (which later turned out not to fit—so is now a gift) and one for Nancy. There seemed to be a constant flow of people into a building, so I went with the flow. People were standing along the wall, usually by themselves, quietly sipping mineral water. There were numerous faucets each with labels next to them, apparently marking the mineral content. As this room was a nightmare to me, not being particularly fond of mineral water, I made a hasty retreat.

The helicopters were ready when we arrived at the "airport" and the Russians were there too, so we departed for unknown lands. All of us have become accustomed to the sounds and shocks of the helicopters, so now we could truly enjoy the countryside without fearing for our lives. And once again we were blessed with an absolutely clear day, and not cold either. As I am sitting here Friday morning in my hotel room looking out at the overcast day, I realize just how fortunate we have been on this trip.

After a long journey southwest of Kislovodsk following the Silk Road, the Valley of the Kyafar River, we dropped down to the highland fortress of the Alans and Khazars. The field upon which we landed was in an isolated setting along the banks of the Kyafar. In a notch in the hills we could see the snow-covered mountains of the Northern Caucasus. These mountains form the boundary between the Northern Caucasus region and the Trans-Caucasus (Southern Caucasus), and we were sitting in the land of the Alanian Tsars' home, the Kyafar Site. A bus was awaiting us to take us along a dirt path and up the various stream beds to the entrance to the site. The bus was small, so it made two trips. How well built it was, and with good springs as our bodies careened off the walls and jostled our breakfast. I had not had a morning repast, so felt only nausea. Ah well.

Our guide at this site was Irina Arzhantseva, a Doctor of History from Moscow University. In addition to her intelligence, she is one of the most attractive women I have ever met. Together with Andrew Belinski's wife, Zvezdana Dode (Dana) we were ensconced in beauty. Irina had been in the field for the past three months with a small field crew and her young daughter. She is deeply admired by her colleagues, not only for her archaeological skills but for her bravery. Just as this site had once been located along a natural route between areas to the south and north, it remains so today. Already there have been armed patrols moving through the area and there is some danger involved. In the months ahead it would not be too surprising to read about some of the towns we have visited in the evening news.

Irina first showed us a series of petroglyphs at the entrance to the fortified town. The town itself dates between the seventh and 10th centuries and was occupied by people who were Christian but who had also maintained much of

Figure 121.
The "deer stones" at the Kyafar site are arranged horizontally or at gentle slants, with pedestals comprised of flat stones beneath them.

their pagan beliefs. And this can be seen in their petroglyphs. Not only are there crosses pecked into the stones, but there are also numerous figures of deer. Deer hunting was apparently a major activity by these people, because their images appear frequently. From one large stone that they recently excavated I copied their forms [Fig. 122]. I am an artist of little worth, but they actually did look like this. One of the stones in the area just excavated had a deep pecked depression in it, which Irina interprets to be a sacrificial altar. She next showed us a cluster of "deer stones" that were arranged horizontal or at a gentle slant. They are in place, as revealed by small pedestals of flat stones that had been arranged beneath them to maintain their position. These too have small circular depressions in them, believed to be of ritual significance.

Figure 122.
Drawn figures of deer petroglyphs at the Kyafar site of the Alanian culture, seventh-10th centuries A.D.

Continuing our climb uphill, we came to a small cliff that could be mounted by climbing a set of stairs. They clearly had been quarried, as they were shaped in blocks. The top of this butte-like area was relatively small, perhaps 20-25 m. in diameter. This was the sanctuary. On one end there was the bare rock with altar stones, again on pedestals, arranged around the summit. In the middle of the summit, and presumably extending to the other end, were the foundations for what is believed to have been a church. This was still being excavated, so we had to be careful how we stepped. An underground entrance once led into this stone structure and, once again, many of the rocks exhibited both Christian and pagan symbols. The altar stones are believed to be earlier than the church, but these were the same people. The Alanians had their own particular brand of Christianity.

After leaving the sanctuary the real climb began. I felt as if I was going to a Middle Woodland "hillfort" in the Midwest U.S.[40] Through the forest, up and up we marched, finally coming to the walls of the fortification. These walls are made of dry stone, and much of the facade remains in excellent shape, especially on the exterior of the fortress. The walls had been about 2 m. broad and in places they are still as much as 3 m. tall. I asked her if she had observed any evolution in the architecture, but they had not yet proceeded to such studies. Although the site has been known since the last century and different parts of the site are recorded, hers is the first systematic excavation. In talking to her later, it is not clear how long she will be able to continue working there because funds are limited and they have to go to sites that are in danger first. Her work is pure research.

The Kyafar fortress is enormous. The walls stretch for about 1 km. along the edge of the hilltop and the enclosed space varies between 300-400 m wide. Including the gate at the bottom of the hill where the "city sign" petroglyph was located, there were once four gates to the city. They probably had cisterns up there, but work has been so limited that they have not yet been detected. I asked Irina if the site was discussed in any of the chronicles and she said that the famous Alanian ruler Durgulel once lived there. He was a prominent leader in the 10th century A.D.

---

40 There is abundant literature on these U.S. sites, but classic examples of the form are Fort Ancient and Fort Hill, both in Ohio. See Ephraim G. Squier and Edwin E. Davis, *Ancient Monuments of the Mississippi Valley*, Smithsonian Contributions to Knowledge 1 (City of Washington: Smithsonian Institution, 1848), Plates 5, 7.

Figure 123.
The Kyafar site sanctuary is situated on top of a small flat butte-like formation. Altar stones occur on one end of the area that bear both pagan and Christian symbols.

Upon descending the hill, we awaited our turn on the "joy bus." This time I stood up and was able to ward off the bumps and blows better. Then it was back on the helicopters and off to Arkhyz, the main Alanian settlement and Christian capital of the area. While waiting for our lunch to be served we had a group picture, first of ourselves, and then with the Russians. Our meal still was not ready, so we walked down to the river to see artifacts and learn something about the site. The river, called Bol Zelencuk, is world famous for reasons having little to do with archaeology. The water is so soft that people from Scotland and Australia sent their wool there in the late 19th–early 20th centuries to wash it without having to use detergents.

Our hostess at the site, Maria Baichorova, Director of the Cherkessk Museum, has been conducting excavations. Unfortunately, none were open at the time, but she did show us various pots, jewelry, glass, and textiles obtained from burial chambers in rocks above the valley. This valley had supported the Alanian capital. Although it is not particularly wide, its value relates to its location along part of the Great Silk route. The gorge has passages that lead directly to the Black Sea, so it was an unavoidable passage to the west from that area. People have long recognized the value of this location, because it was occupied for several millennia before the fifth/sixth centuries A.D. when the Alanians first appeared. The city was destroyed during the Tatar/Mongolian invasion and it was not occupied again until the 18th/19th centuries when people started to return. During the Crimean War its archaeological significance was beginning to be recognized, but it has only been recently that it has been designated a cultural monument. As with the Tatar site, up to two years ago there were still squatters at the site. The archaeologists have been living in and restoring the various 18th/19th century structures in what had been a monastery up until the Bolshevik Revolution, but their work has been slow and tedious, and they apologized for it not being better. They certainly had no reason to apologize. I have been so impressed with what strides they have been able to make with so few funds and labor so minimal. For all of these archaeologists, what they do is truly a labor of love and that message comes through in the presentations of their work. They are very proud of their country and are desperate to let the world know of its significance.[41]

The lunch—a totally inappropriate word. Dinner does no justice to it either. Feast is the proper term. I know of no other word to describe it. We ate outside at one continuous table with benches arranged at both sides. Appetizers consisted of homemade (what else?) dill pickles and 10% beer (!). We were warned to take it easy on the beer, but few listened to the advice. Next we were given large tin bowls and slices of freshly baked bread that looked like the tops of giant mushrooms before slicing. The preparers of this sumptuous meal then appeared behind Sherry, who was opposite me, and plunked in her bowl the leg of a lamb, about 5 lbs. worth. Her eyes were like saucers when she saw what was before her and they explained that the principal cut always goes to the leader, who in their experience usually was a male. She could not have the particular part they would give him so they gave her a piece that only females could eat. We did not obtain the rest of the story, but obviously we were curious. Sherry shared parts of her dish with others, including men, so we're probably all cursed. There didn't need to be any sharing though, because we were all doled out portions that were comparable with Sherry's. I had a rib that was over a foot long and we were all then given a saucer-sized potato-pancake that was to be eaten with gobs of

---

41 For a more recent contribution to our understanding of archaeology in the Kislovodosk Basin, see Dmitry Korobov, "Early Medieval Settlement in Southern Russia: Changing Directions," *Medieval Archaeology* 56, no. 1 (2012): 34-59.

Figure 124.
The delegation was treated to an Alanian Feast at the Arkhyz settlement. This was the main Alanian settlement and the Christian capital of the region between the fifth/sixth centuries A.D. and the Tatar invasion of the 13th century.

butter. What really made this a true Alanian feast is that there were no knives nor napkins of any sort, so we certainly did look the beast after the main course. But of course we were not finished. Out came the large vat of fermented goat's milk, a true delicacy in these parts. All of us were ladled a large cup of this cold, white-colored, lumpy mixture that tasted like a cross between yogurt gone bad and cottage cheese gone bad. I downed my brew, the perfect (probably stupid) guest, and thought that was it, but then the soup came out. I thought that would do me in, but it actually quieted my stomach. It was the broth that the lamb had boiled in and it was seasoned perfectly. Watermelon slices completed the meal and almost finished us all. For some it was just too much. Poor Maria Azzi,[42] she was lying on the ground, not so much from the size of the meal, but from the cultural shock of it. The feast, the food preparation and service, were so different from her Argentinian roots that she literally was in shock and had become sick. I can understand. It was certainly very different from anything I had ever had, but it was still within the "southern barbecue" tradition.

---

42   At the time of our trip to Russia, Ms. Azzi was a Social Anthropologist–Researcher at the Institute of Anthropological Investigations in Buenos Aires.

Figure 125.
People to People
delegates and our
Russian hosts at the
Arkhyz settlement.

With the meal complete and hearty toasts made to the hosts and hostesses, we made our departures. Curiously, the helicopters were a bit slow in rising, but they finally emerged from the Alanian capital and we began our trip home. We hugged the edge of the snow-capped Caucasus as we traveled due west, and then turned 90 degrees to advance to Kislovodsk. We were all exhausted when we landed, but not too exhausted because we decided to shop in town for about an hour before going home. I walked around the various vendors who had shoes, sweaters, and various other odds and ends arranged wherever they could acquire space—on the benches, on the ground, anywhere. They had never seen an American and when they finally recognized me for what I was they clustered all around me trying to sell me one thing or another. Some sweater ladies who looked like sisters actually followed me back to the bus and set up shop nearby awaiting the return of my comrades. They ended up doing alright. I actually bought another hat for Nancy from them and, from another shop in the colonnade area I bought a Russian/English dictionary.

It was about dark by the time we were back on the bus and when we finally got to the hotel we had less than an hour to prepare for the banquet. Within that time I not only had to get washed and dressed, but I had to wrap six or seven presents so I was pretty busy. We drove to a nearby night club for the banquet and, once again, it was a truly memorable experience with our Russian colleagues. I spent a lot of time talking with Yuri Litvinenko. We had talked many times during the trip. He and the people in his Institute are very anxious in collaborating with museums in the States on exhibits from their region, as well as lectures. Paul (Bristo) and Sherry asked me if I might be interested in pursuing such a relationship with them, and I said I'd be more than happy to do so. I think the Alabama Museum of Natural History would be excited about the possibility of staging a Scythian exhibit and of hosting Russian archaeologists for a lecture tour. I told Yuri that I would do what I can do and that we would remain in touch. I also promised to send him a set of Indian slides, which I will do when I get home. We exchanged gifts. He gave me a replica of a silver Scythian style bowl to be used as a sugar cup, and I gave him a series of articles and a small bound book of blank pages for whatever purpose he desired.

I ate very little at the banquet as most of my time was spent doling out gifts, thanking people, and just talking. I spent a lot of time speaking with both Irina and Dana (I am a sucker for pretty women) and drinking vodka with my old drinking buddies Yuri and Albert. Albert was surprised to see a professor tipsy, but I told him it was just his imagination. Yuri good-naturedly "ridiculed" my vodka sipping and expounded upon the joys of drinking it promptly, and I'm afraid that I paid too much attention to his lecture and downed a few in proper Russian fashion. Did I mention the dancing girls? They came on, three to be exact with one male who could have been eliminated, and showed us their wares for about half an hour. Some of the delegation apparently were annoyed by the disruption, but I thought it an excellent opportunity to study the music and dance of another's culture. Ethnography is a tough job, but somebody has to do it.

With much hugs and kisses (men-women, men-men, women-women, etc.), we closed up the night club a little past midnight. Igor kept yelling that we had to leave and after the fifth yell we decided we had best escort Igor out if our departure actually was going to take place. Irina and Dana had their two little children all nestled in the coach, reminding me of my precious offspring, and with peals of laughter borne of friendship and cultural exchange, we made our way

Figure 126.
The author and his new friends at the Essentuky banquet, a fitting ending. From left: Ian W. Brown, Yuri Litvinenko, Irina Arzhantseva, and Zvezdana Dode (Dana).

home. Albert warned us all to walk straight as they do not permit inebriated persons in the hotel, so I sucked in my breath, negotiated what had become an extremely narrow gate, made a gesture of recognition to the doorman, and proceeded to trip my way up the stairs. I do not remember going to sleep, but I awoke the next morning with a terrible head, undoubtedly due to the sumptuous feast and the incessant levity of my companions.

TODAY WAS THE BEGINNING OF THE END. I AM SAD IT IS FINISHING, BUT AT THE PACE we have been going if it doesn't end soon, I will. I could not go to breakfast, for various reasons, so slept a little later than usual. I packed my gear and wrote until 11:30 a.m., at which time we were all to have our luggage in the lobby. As usual, it was a hurry up and wait event, but this has been characteristic of the trip overall and is just a fact of life in traveling through Russia. Our new Russian friends rode with us to the airport at Mineralnye Vody and we visited with them before departing. We were outside for quite a while waiting for our bags to be loaded, and just before leaving, a man with a dark complexion ambled up to me. He wore a raggedy suit and had a wool hat atop his head, reminding me of some folks I had seen in New York not too long ago. He got fairly close to me and gently nodded his head. I nodded mine too and he smiled showing a mouth full of gold fillings. I smiled too and again nodded my head. He did likewise and we must have looked like fools. Finally he said "American?" I said "Da" and after a while I pointed at the ground and said, "You live here?" He looked confused and then said, "Tashkent, Uzbekistan." I said "Ah, yes" in recognition, as I remembered some important sites from that area. He said again, "America," and I said "Yes, New York" thinking that he might recognize that. He did and smiled again, followed by the now-expected "America." After the third repetition he said "America—dollar" and I now understood my new friend's motive. I shook my head, reached in my pocket and pulled out 100 rubles and he, in turn, shook his head and said "Dollar." I couldn't give the rubles away! We both smiled again, nodded our heads and separated, me and my friend from Uzbekistan who are no wiser now about each other's lives than we were 10 minutes previous. However, I did have an appreciation of the value of the American dollar.

The flight was perfect, at least in terms of the actual physical flying. I would have been happy to exterminate the music though, as it drove me crazy. The repetitious, high-pitched caterwauling sounded like the Russian version of the "Chipmunks" and it just kept going on and on. However, we finally did land and during the flight I managed to read about 50 pages or so in *The Don*, so it was relaxing for the most part. After about an hour in the airport, we drove into St.

Return to St. Petersburg.

The man from Tashkent.

A now familiar landscape.

Petersburg and checked into the Okhtinskaya Hotel, a very ritzy hotel that was built about two years ago.

On the way to the hotel I kept my nose to the window, taking in the road, cars, and buildings of St. Petersburg. It now seems familiar. Dirt was everywhere—the cars, the streets, the buildings all have thick layers of dust—but now it didn't seem so offensive. As I looked in the cars or in the gaily lit rooms, I saw people, Russian people. I didn't remember seeing them, or at least focusing on them when I arrived a couple of weeks ago. Even though I met only a few Russians in my time here, through them I have been able to appreciate the other nameless faces, to look beyond the decay and see people who are just like me in so many ways. But I was still behind glass. My nose was pressed against it to be sure, and I was genuinely interested in the scenes outside the bus, but I was still within the bus. Wherever we have gone we have been behind glass. Whether in airports, hotels, or museums, our location was always accounted for. This was necessary and ensured our security, but it also made us travelers rather than inhabitants. I do not and cannot pretend to know the Russians. A lifetime would be necessary, and even then I'm not sure I would understand the complexity of their culture, but these two weeks have given me an appreciation of the complexity of their lives in the past and present, and for that alone it has been a memorable trip.

NEW YORK NEVER LOOKED SO GOOD TO ME. WE FLEW OUT OF ST. PETERSBURG IN the morning, with a short stop in Helsinki. There was no trouble with customs in Russia and even less problems getting through New York. No one had their baggage checked in New York, which was a surprise to all and an indication of the power and/or respect of the People to People organization. As we, about 15 of us, stood outside the terminal waiting for our shuttle bus to the Holiday Inn, we were surrounded by a horde of Puerto Rican nationalists welcoming a dignitary. Flags waved and bouquets of flowers were thrown as the elderly man was hustled into the limousine. The crowd then dispersed as other groups took their place. The sun was shining, the air was warm, and the streets were clean. As we drove to the hotel, I noted the trim landscape, the color, and the smiles of the people—alive with energy and enthusiasm. On the news we learned that H. Ross Perot had thrown his lot back into the Presidential race, a blow to the two-party system, but no threat to the design and operation of our political structure. We also learned that the value of the ruble had dropped even further. In the space of two weeks its value, relative to the dollar, had decreased by 50%. We complain of our economy, we rant and rave about our politics, but I will never do so again without a feeling of guilt. Travel allows perspective for one's lot in life and provides humility. Prior to visiting Russia I was much more confident in my views. Although I traveled behind glass, in bus, plane, or helicopter, the windows were clean, and my vision was clear. I see much more now than I did two weeks previous, and I will never again be the same.

October 3, 1992
(Saturday)

New York revisited, a new perspective.

CPSIA information can be obtained
at www.ICGtesting.com
Printed in the USA
BVHW090446101020
590728BV00001B/2

9 781734 573046